Praise for
Silently Seduced, Revised and Updated

"For the past twenty years, *Silently Seduced* has been the comprehensive guidebook on the subject of covert incest for both the clinician and the layperson seeking insight into this difficult-to-identify issue. With this updated edition, Dr. Adams has brought new and timely insights to the subject, expanding discussion of the issue to include a broader range of relationships—one that reflects the more complicated world we live in."

—Eleanor D. Payson, LMSW, author of
The Wizard of Oz and Other Narcissists

"Dr. Adams expertly sheds light on a critical issue that is, sadly, romanticized by Hollywood and insufficiently deconstructed in clinical training programs. This book is a must read for men and women experiencing compulsive sexual and romantic pain, parents interested in raising healthy children, and clinicians who want to offer sensitive, informed support along the way."

—Kelly McDaniel, psychotherapist and author of
Ready to Heal: Women Facing Love, Sex, and Relationship Addiction

"Like the original *Silently Seduced*, Dr. Ken Adams's updated version is engaging, clear, and hopeful. It adds new insights and guidance that makes this new edition a compelling read for those in need and professionals alike."

—John C. Friel, Ph.D., and Linda Friel, M.A., authors of
Adult Children: The Secrets of Dysfunctional Families and
An Adult Child's Guide to What's "Normal"

"In this welcome new edition of his classic book, Adams perceptively expands his earlier work, and in a nuanced way explains much more about the subtleties of covert abuse and its aftereffects."

—Richard Gartner, Ph.D., author of *Beyond Betrayal*
and past president of MaleSurvivor.org.

"This groundbreaking recovery classic shines a compassionate light on the hidden world of covert incest. Dr. Adams's poignant stories and clinical wisdom empower readers to recognize dysfunctional relationships, heal long-standing emotional wounds, and create an intimate life of their own choosing."

—Wendy Maltz, LCSW, D.S.T., author of
The Sexual Healing Journey and coauthor of *The Porn Trap*

"*Silently Seduced* is a must read for those who have difficulty establishing and maintaining romantic relationships. It gives the reader the keys to understanding how covert incest in childhood stands in the way of having an adult, healthy, intimate relationship and offers the hope of a new beginning. Dr. Adams so thoroughly 'nails' the problem that *Silently Seduced* is a stand-alone book on the topic."

—Alexandra Katehakis, M.F.T., author of *Erotic Intelligence*

"The confusing and complex conflicts experienced by the child who is filling in for what is missing in the parent's relationship are explored with expertise, and Adams does a compelling job of delineating how these conflicts play out as these 'little partners' enter their own, adult relationships."

—Tian Dayton, Ph.D., author of
Emotional Sobriety

"Kenneth Adams has done it again! As in the original *Silently Seduced*, Dr. Adams eloquently speaks to the source of so many adults' chronic struggles with intimacy. This revised edition uses powerful anecdotes to bring well-organized theoretical perspectives to life, creating a highly readable, deeply moving experience for readers. The Q&A at the end of the book effectively creates the experience of a personal conversation with Dr. Adams. We cannot wait to begin using this revised edition as a powerful treatment resource with our clients!"

—Ginger Bercaw, Psy.D., CSAT, CST, and Bill Bercaw, Psy.D., CSAT, CST,
authors of *The Couple's Guide to Intimacy* and
From the Living Room to the Bedroom.

"This book is a must read for anyone looking to understand or heal from incestuous relationships. Dr. Adams's raw and in-depth look brings clarity to a controversial topic. By answering the 'why' and the 'how,' readers can gain new insight to process their emotions and make important changes in their lives and relationships."

—Stefanie Carnes, Ph.D., LMFT, author of
Mending a Shattered Heart

"*Silently Seduced* offers precious insight into some of the least understood and most hidden of men's emotional challenges."

—Robert Weiss, LCSW, CSAT-S, founding director of The Sexual Recovery Institute and author of *Cruise Control* and *Untangling the Web*

"*Silently Seduced* is a necessary tool for all therapists who work with survivors of overt or covert incest as well as the client who has even a slight dysfunctional relationship with a parent or family member. The book includes great case examples that are easily relatable and would benefit anyone struggling with an inappropriate relationship with a parent—some that most may not even see as inappropriate until reading this book."

—Erin A. Munroe, author of *When Big Issues Happen to Little Girls*

"*Silently Seduced* is a book [we] here at PCS recommend to therapists and to our clients. No one has done a better job at dealing with covert incest in the manner that speaks clearly to therapists and clients and provides helpful information in terms of 'what to do.'"

—Ralph H. Earle, Ph.D., founder and president of
Psychological Counseling Services, Ltd.

"*Silently Seduced* offers much-needed validation for anyone who has been held hostage by a parent's inappropriate need for companionship. Dr. Adams speaks to the overwhelming responsibility placed on a child who becomes the surrogate partner for a needy, lonely parent and explores how this burden interferes in normal development, which results in later struggles for intimacy, healthy sexuality, and commitment. He offers help and hope for anyone who has been the victim of covert incest and greater understanding for those in the helping professions."

—Jane Middleton-Moz, M.S., coauthor of *After the Tears: Helping Adult
Children of Alcoholics Heal Their Childhood Trauma*

SILENTLY SEDUCED

REVISED & UPDATED

When Parents Make Their Children Partners

Kenneth M. Adams, Ph.D.
Foreword by Patrick J. Carnes, Ph.D.

Health Communications, Inc.
Deerfield Beach, Florida

www.hcibooks.com

Library of Congress Cataloging-in-Publication Data

Adams, Kenneth M., 1955-
   Silently seduced : when parents make their children partners /
Kenneth M. Adams.—Rev. & updated ed.
      p. cm.
Includes bibliographical references and index.
ISBN-13: 978-0-7573-1587-9 (trade paper)
ISBN-10: 0-7573-1587-9 (trade paper)
ISBN-13: 978-0-7573-9174-3 (e-book)
ISBN-10: 0-7573-9174-5 (e-book)
   1. Incest victims—Psychology.   2. Adult child sexual abuse victims—
Psychology.   1. Title.
HV6570.6.A33 2011
306.877—dc23

                                                                2011024018

Publisher: Health Communications, Inc.
3201 S.W. 15th Street
Deerfield Beach, FL 33442-8190

Cover design by Larissa Hise Henoch
Inside design and formatting by Dawn Von Strolley Grove

To Cheryl and Zachary,
the loves and joys of my life.

Also by Kenneth M. Adams, Ph.D.

When He's Married to Mom:
How to Help Mother-Enmeshed Men
Open Their Hearts to True Love and Commitment
(with Alexander P. Morgan)

Clinical Management of Sex Addiction
(with Patrick J. Carnes, Ph.D.)

Contents

∽⬥∾

Foreword

WE ARE FORTUNATE when a gifted clinician drills down into a specific problem many have, and then writes about it in a way most of us can make sense of it. When Ken Adams's *Silently Seduced* first appeared, the book became an instant classic by providing recovering people the links and insights that help make sense of unfathomable incongruities. In therapy, we learn to watch the patterns of the mind, first to stop dysfunctional behavior and then to construct new and reengineered thinking patterns leading to sexual and relationship satisfaction. For many, *Silently Seduced* was key in that process.

Within the field of sex addiction, Ken Adams focuses on the set of dynamics that many sex addicts find true to their patterns. Loving a person but not being able to be sexual with that partner is a great irony when sex is easy with anonymous or unavailable partners. Moreover, sex is often driven by an anger for which we use the term *eroticized rage*. Sex addicts are aware of the sexual arousal but oblivious to how their behavior is angry. Further, why there would be such anger is a mystery to them, given that they felt so cared for as children. In *Silently Seduced*, the anatomy of how this happens is laid out in a way that is so helpful.

Dr. Adams followed up *Silently Seduced* with his book *When*

He Is Married to Mom, which looked more closely into the issues involved with the mother bond. Taken together, these books have been a literal godsend to patients and a resource to therapists.

This new version of *Silently Seduced* is an enriched and insightful edition of an already successful book and updates the original content with new findings, expanded discussions of key points, and a section of frequently asked questions. It adds insight and clarity to the topics of women who were their mothers' surrogate companions, gay men, single parents, and spouses or partners of covert incest survivors. Dr. Adams also expands his discussion regarding overcoming the fear of commitment, setting boundaries, and how best to handle dating and new relationships. For those of us who are book watchers, we note those who work for continuous improvement and model integrity, both as authors and clinicians. That is the way I have always known Ken Adams to be: thoughtful, thorough, and insightful. His books are always worth the effort of a careful read.

—Patrick Carnes, Ph.D.

Introduction to the Revised and Updated Edition

WHEN I BEGAN writing *Silently Seduced* twenty years ago, I could not have imagined its longevity and impact. Since then, hundreds of covert incest survivors have discussed the book with me in therapy sessions and have mentioned it in lectures. They most frequently report two main reactions to the book: one, that it clarifies a troublesome parent-child relationship history that was perplexing and previously beyond the reader's understanding; and two, that the succinct and clear manner in which it is written allows readers to be undistracted by repetition or material that is spurious to the topic. As such, *Silently Seduced* has not only been informative to its readers, but transformative as well. For many, it opened an emotional, experiential moment that ignited the search for more clarity and healing.

Over the years, I have received many important and thoughtful questions that the original text did not adequately answer. For example, some readers are still seeking clarity on why I consider it incestuous when a parent turns a child into a surrogate husband or wife but does not touch them sexually. Others have sought more information on how best to manage their adult relationship with their parent. They want to neither continue with the same level of inappropriate closeness nor completely "divorce" their parent.

Other questions have been about how to deal with siblings, how to date, and how to handle the tension between the intrusive parent and the romantic partner. Readers have wanted more perspective on emotional issues, such as how to break free from the suffocating guilt or fear of engulfment that seems to plague covert incest survivors so often. A desire for a healthy relationship and a way to finally feel contented in love is the source of many questions. Wanting to understand why their sexuality seems so burdened, even though there was no sexual touch, creates a frequent source of confusion for survivors.

I've also been asked about certain populations or special circumstances. For example, are there different issues for a gay man who is involved as a surrogate husband to his mother than for a straight man? What about when a daughter plays the role of a surrogate partner to her mother as opposed to her father? Are there implications for single-parent households or for adults who choose to have and raise a child as a single parent? What are the specific problems and concerns for the partners or spouses of covert incest survivors? How should they best respond to the difficulties in their relationships caused by the covert incest of their partners?

Although many survivors of covert incest are able to relate to the stories of overt incest survivors, most struggle to feel validated because they have not been physically violated. Covert incest survivors are still suffering in silence. In fact, most are not aware that their relationships with their parents were incestuous.

I've written this book to give such survivors a framework to understand what happened to them, how their lives continue to be affected, and how to begin the process of recovery.

What follows in this new edition is an update to the original text and a new chapter that addresses the questions that have emerged over the last twenty years. The new chapter, Frequently Asked Questions, is a dialogue between you, the reader, and me, as if we were sitting down in a therapy session or I was responding during a lecture. In addition, new material has emerged in the field over the years that supports my observations. The bibliography has been updated to reflect those sources.

In the first part of the book, I use the word "victim" to describe the person still experiencing the effects of covert incest. These early chapters describe the victimization process and its consequences. In the last chapters, I discuss change and recovery. I use the word "survivor" instead of "victim" at that point to help underscore the important transformation from being a victim to reclaiming life. Also, to help the stories flow without the encumbering use of he/she or him/her, I use personal pronouns interchangeably.

The stories presented in the book are composites designed to illustrate the traits of covert incest survivors. Your actual experience may vary. No one story represents any one person's particular life. To protect their right to privacy, I have purposely avoided using the stories of my clients. However, their sharing certainly has influenced my thinking. To that extent, there may be some overlap between what I have heard in my practice and what I have included in these pages. I am grateful to my clients for the sharing of their lives and the trust they have given me in the process. I respect their courage.

As I did in the original book, I strive to be clear and to the point, with as little psychological jargon as possible, in hopes that the new edition becomes another transformative step in your journey from pain and struggle to healing and freedom.

What Is the Silent Seduction?

*As long as the child within is not allowed to become aware of
what happened to him or her, a part of his or her emotional
life will remain frozen . . . all appeals to love, solidarity, and
compassion will be useless.*

—Alice Miller, *For Your Own Good*

TOM CAME HOME from a long day at the office and was
looking forward to the quiet, intimate dinner he and his wife
had planned. The telephone rang. It was his mother. *Now what?*
he thought. He listened as she described her day. Eventually, she
began discussing how lonely and miserable she felt with Tom's
father. Tom felt his rage boil but was paralyzed by his guilt. He
looked for an opening in her tirade so he could politely excuse
himself and eat his dinner, which was waiting for him.

How do I get out of this one? Tom thought as his mother went on describing her feelings of sexual dissatisfaction with his father. Impatient and outraged, he paced the floor and hoped his mother would hang up.

When she said, "I don't know what I would do if I didn't have you. I wish your father would listen to me like you do," Tom had had enough. He hung up without a word and threw the phone to the floor in a rage. Teary-eyed, he screamed to his wife, "I don't want to know about her personal problems! I hate it, but I don't know what to do." As had happened so many times before, Tom's evening with his wife was ruined.

As a therapist, I've learned Tom's story is not unique. Frequently, I hear comments such as, "I can't stand it when my dad keeps telling me how much he loves his 'little princess,'" or "I wish my mom would stop telling me about her loneliness. It's not my business," or "I know my dad doesn't mean anything by it, but it feels funny when he seems so worried about how I dress and gets jealous when I go out with men." The list is endless, but the theme is the same: a sense of violation and a boundary crossed. These violations are usually done in the name of loving and caring.

There is nothing loving or caring about a close parent-child relationship when it services the needs and feelings of the parent rather than the child. "Feeling close" with your parents, particularly the opposite-sex parent, is not the source of comfort the image suggests. It is a relationship in which the individual, both as a child and later as an adult, feels silently seduced by the parent. Feelings of appreciation and gratitude do not prevail in these "close" relationships. Instead, they are a source of confusing, progressive rage.

During the feedback section of my lectures on the subject, some participants are quite vocal with their rage. They express relief that they now understand why at times they hate with vengeance the same parent who has always loved them "so much." Some are frozen in their seats and can't speak, while others can't wait to leave. A few courageous parents speak up, expressing that they are now beginning to understand why their sons or daughters struggle in relationships.

Others listen to the lectures and insist there is no harm in their close relationship with their opposite-sex parent. Actually, they claim to feel special and privileged. These children were given a special position by being idealized by the parent. But there is no privilege in being cheated out of a childhood by being a parent's surrogate partner. As adults, these individuals in turn idealize their parents to cover the pain of the abandoned and victimized child within. To be a parent's surrogate partner is to be a victim of covert incest. This book is about the silent seduction covert incest victims experience and its effect on their sexuality, intimacy, and relationships.

Throughout most of the book I use examples of the covert incest survivor with his or her opposite-sex parent. This better illuminates the inappropriate sexual and romantic tension created by covert incest. However, a child can also be the surrogate partner of the same-sex parent. In chapters four and eight, I address issues specific to covert incest that involve the same-sex parent.

Being a parent's surrogate partner as a child, and continuing to be one as an adult, has a profound effect on one's life. If you find yourself in the following descriptions, this book is for you.

Common Characteristics of Silent Seduction

A Love/Hate Relationship. You often have intense feelings of both love and hate for the opposite-sex parent. On the one hand, you feel special and privileged because of the relationship; on the other, you frequently feel you aren't doing enough for that parent. This conflict causes feelings of guilt that result in rage, which is seldom expressed directly.

Emotional Distance from Same-Sex Parent. In contrast to the love/hate relationship with the opposite-sex parent, you feel abandoned by the same-sex parent. This relationship is often competitive, and the parent feels like an adversary. Feeling contempt for this parent is common.

Guilt and Confusion over Personal Needs. You feel guilty about your needs and probably have a difficult time identifying what they are. You generally try to "be strong," caretake, or always "be there" for others as a way of meeting your own needs.

Feelings of Inadequacy. You are likely to have chronic feelings of inadequacy and unworthiness. You believe your worth as a man or woman is determined by what you can do rather than by who you are.

Multiple Relationships. You are likely to have been in and out of many relationships and never felt satisfied. You are always on the lookout for the perfect partner or relationship. Establishing intimacy is difficult for you.

Difficulty with Commitment. You are generally ambivalent about commitment in relationships. You always seem to have one foot in and one foot out of the door, just in case.

Hasty Commitments. You make a quick commitment to a relationship then realize later it was not a good choice. You feel too guilty to leave, and you try to make it right instead.

Regret over Past Relationships. You find yourself looking back at a previous relationship and wondering if it could have worked if you had stuck it out.

Sexual Dysfunction. You find yourself feeling sexually shut down or driven and compulsive in the pursuit of sexual highs or conquests. Sex may become addictive.

Compulsions/Addictions. You have other compulsions or addictions. You may be driven in the areas of work, success, and achievement. You may find yourself addicted to food, either compulsively overeating, starving yourself, or binging and purging.

2

When a Child Is Betrayed
by a Parent's Love

Your children . . . are the sons and daughters of Life's longing
for itself. They come through you but not from you, And
though they are with you yet they belong not to you.

—Khalil Gibran, *The Prophet*

INCEST CONFUSES AND STIRS US. The word is usually used
to describe sexual contact between a parent and child. *Webster's
New World Dictionary* defines incest as "sexual intercourse between persons too closely related to marry legally." There are both
overt and covert forms of incest.

Overt Incest

Overt incest occurs when there is sexual contact in any dependent relationship involving blood relatives, the most obvious being between parent and child. A more inclusive definition is given by Mike Lew in *Victims No Longer* where he states, "Incest is a violation of a position of trust, power, and protection." It is the dependency in these relationships that is exploited by the adult for their sexual needs that crosses the incestuous line. As we shall discuss later, this is the same dependency that is leveraged by the parent to turn a child into a surrogate partner.

Sexual contact in dependent relationships is never justifiable because there is always a loss of choice. People in dependent relationships seldom challenge those in positions of authority, even when they feel victimized and violated. This is especially true when the violation is between parent and child. One of the ways parents justify their behavior is to believe, "This is my child, so I can do what I want."

Children are not property. They feel terrified and degraded when a parent, or any adult, is sexual with them. Cooperation does not equal enjoyment. They are too scared, too emotionally needy, or too starved for affection to say no. Even if children report that at some level they enjoyed the sexual contact, it is still emotionally damaging. Children are generally too needy and confused to understand inappropriate sexual touch. Their enjoyment is, at some level, a source of guilt and shame later in life: "It was my fault because I enjoyed it and didn't say no. All my life I carried guilt because I thought I seduced my father. It wasn't until I went over the wreckage of my life that I realized I was a victim of incest."

Historically, most reports of overt incest involved girls. However, many boys have been sexually violated by both women and men. Unfortunately, instances of boys being violated have been underreported. This is beginning to change, thanks to the efforts of groups like Male Survivor. (See appendix and bibliography for resources and books about sexually abused boys.) Reported cases generally involve an adult man with a boy; however, many boys report being sexually violated by their mothers, stepmothers, aunts, female neighbors, and babysitters. Sexual stereotypes about men contribute to the underreporting of boys who are incest victims. For example, the myth that "men are just more sexual than women and always want sex" suggests a young boy would welcome being sexually stimulated by an adult woman and would not necessarily feel victimized. On the contrary, a young boy just learning about his body and sexuality is overwhelmed to have a woman touch him in a sexual way.

One man described his shame and confusion during his childhood relationship with his mother:

My mother always insisted on washing my genitals, even when I was old enough to do it myself. Sometimes it was embarrassing; other times I enjoyed it. I didn't know what to think. Sometimes she'd give me kisses on the lips that seemed to last too long. I would often find myself sexually aroused when I looked at her. I privately felt I was strange, and I worried that someone would find out. To this day I feel like I was some kind of pervert, because I was sexually aroused by my mother's presence.

A victim of overt incest commonly reacts by internalizing fault—in other words, the victim feels responsible for what occurred. This internalization of fault or guilt inhibits healthy expression of anger. Instead, self-hatred festers. The expression of anger is necessary, however, in the healing and letting go process of an incest victim.

Overt incest is one of the most frightening and traumatic experiences a young girl or boy has to endure. A common myth is that overt incest is the exception rather than the rule in American families. This is not the case. The National Center for the Victims of Crime reports that one in four girls and one in six boys will have experienced an episode of sexual abuse by the time they are eighteen years of age. Another myth is that most sexual abuse is perpetrated by strangers or nonfamily members. In fact, according to Childhelp, 68 percent of all childhood sexual abuse is committed by family members.

Yet, as traumatic and injurious as overt incest is, healing is possible if adults are gently guided and supported through the pain and into expression of their feelings. Victims have to be encouraged to express anger and separate from the shame and guilt. They need to be reassured that they did not cause the incest. Over time, this approach helps victims grieve the loss of their sexual innocence. Experiencing the sadness and shedding tears permit a cleansing from the incest experience. In its place grows comfortableness with one's sexuality and the hope for a healthy sexual future.

Generally, incest victims who do not recover are the ones who keep the experience a secret, deny it ever occurred, or minimize its effects. In these cases, comments frequently include statements like: "Well, it only happened once . . . maybe a couple of times," or "It's easier just to forget about it." As a result, the victim remains stuck in the guilt and shame. This contributes to dissatisfying intimate and sexual relationships.

Victims need support and appropriate professional guidance to recover from the violation. Incest victims (both as children and adults) who report their experiences to a helping professional (therapist, doctor, clergy, nurse, or teacher) may find they are not believed. Worse, they are sometimes accused of being the seducer. This furthers the shame and is another violation. Appropriate professional guidance that does not further the shame is available and should be sought. Support groups such as Incest Survivors Anonymous and Survivors of Incest Anonymous are available for help. (See appendix for listings of these and other support groups.)

If children are discounted by a helping professional or any adult, they fall into deep despair. Helping professionals must be willing to follow through and intervene when necessary. A helping professional who receives a report of incest and consciously chooses not to take appropriate action participates in the victimizing process. This is also true if a child goes to one parent complaining that the other is sexually abusive. For that parent to minimize or deny the violation is to become a participant in the incest. The child is being abused by both parents through the direct sexual contact of one and the failure to protect of the other.

Covert Incest

Victims of covert incest, also referred to as emotional incest, suffer pain similar to that of overt victims. Understanding covert incest as a sexual violation is less clear, since direct sexual contact does not occur. This is not to imply that it is easy to identify or sort feelings of overt incest: it is not. However, similar feelings and dynamics are at work with covert incest. Although estimated numbers of overt incest victims exist, similar statistics are not available regarding covert victims. The numbers are potentially staggering, since the possibility for covert incest exists anytime a chronic break occurs in the emotional, spiritual, or sexual bond between parents.

Covert incest occurs when a child becomes the object of a parent's affection, love, passion, and preoccupation. The parent, motivated by the loneliness and emptiness created by a chronically troubled marriage or relationship, makes the child a surrogate partner. The boundary between caring love and incestuous love is crossed when the relationship with the child exists to meet the needs of the parent rather than those of the child. As the deterioration in the marriage progresses, the dependency on the child grows, and the opposite-sex parent's response to the child becomes increasingly characterized by desperation, jealousy, and a disregard for personal boundaries. The child becomes an object to be manipulated and used so the parent can avoid the pain and reality of a troubled marriage.

The child feels used and trapped; these are the same feelings overt incest victims experience. Attempts at play, autonomy, and friendship render the child guilt-ridden and lonely, never able to feel okay about his or her needs. Over time, the child becomes preoccupied with the parent's needs and feels protective and concerned. A psychological marriage between parent and child results; the child becomes the parent's surrogate spouse.

A healthy emotional, sexual, and spiritual bond between parents creates an unspoken, unseen boundary that properly channels sexual feelings and energies. When a child grows up in a family in which the marriage is chronically disturbed, sexual feelings and energy are never put into perspective. To the child, the parent's love feels more confining than freeing, more demanding than giving, and more intrusive than nurturing. The relationship becomes sexually energized and violating, even without the presence of sexual innuendos, sexual touch, or conscious sexual feelings on the part of the parent. The chronic lack of attachment in the marriage is enough to create an atmosphere of sexualized energy that spills over to the child.

The sexual energy or tension created in a relationship of covert incest is more akin to young love than to a caring parent-child love. Eric described his story of growing up with an alcoholic father and a mother who kept him close.

> *My mother and I fought a lot, but I would have killed anyone who put their hands on her—including my father. Sometimes I had fits of jealous rage when she paid more attention to my father or some other man. She was mine and I wasn't going to share her.*

Monica described her experience this way:

I always felt special being Daddy's girl, especially when he brought home presents just for me and no one else. I wanted to be with him wherever he went; I was so in love with my daddy.

There is an important difference between overt and covert incest: while the overt victim feels abused, the covert victim feels *idealized* and *privileged*. Yet, underneath the thin mask of feeling special and privileged rests the same trauma of the overt victim: rage, anger, shame, and guilt. The sense of exploitation resulting from being a parent's surrogate partner or spouse is buried behind a wall of illusion and denial. The adult covert incest victim remains stuck in a pattern of living that is aimed at keeping the special relationship going with the opposite-sex parent. It is a pattern of always trying to please mommy or daddy. In this way, the adult continues to be idealized. A privileged and special position is maintained, and the pain and suffering of a lost childhood are denied. Separation never occurs, and feelings of being trapped in the psychological marriage deepen. This interferes with the victim's capacity for healthy intimacy and sexuality.

James's description of his divorce is a common story.

Ann just got fed up with me putting my mother before her. We would be enjoying a Sunday, our only day off together. My mother would call, and I would run right over there. I knew it was hurting my marriage, but I couldn't stand the guilt of not doing what my mother wanted. I felt trapped. Then I'd get angry with my wife and accuse her of being selfish when she complained. Finally, Ann divorced me. I never understood my relationship with my mother was so damaging. It always felt good being Mom's "man of the house." My feelings for her used to be special to me, but now I only feel guilty, confused, and angry.

Consider Bonnie's story. A bright, attractive, forty-year-old professional, she can't understand why she has never married, despite wanting to.

As I started dating, I kept bringing men home for my dad to approve of, but he never did. I went through one relationship after another. I felt I would never find a man as good as my daddy. So my relationships became less and less meaningful and exclusively sexual. I became addicted to sex. When I began to need to be physically abused to be sexually aroused, I finally sought help. I had traveled far astray from my original dream of getting married to a man as good as Daddy. During therapy I learned that Daddy's special love for me actually left me feeling ashamed and angry. I had no idea being Daddy's little girl wasn't normal and set me up for a life of pain and loneliness.

These stories and similar ones are told by men and women who have been their parents' partners. The seduction inherent in these psychological marriages is subtle and insidious, as is its effect on one's capacity for a fulfilling sexual and intimate life. Since the parent-child relationship is used to meet the needs of the parent in the psychological marriage, the child feels ashamed of legitimate needs and fears displeasing the parent. As unhealthy as it is, the child has no choice but to actively participate in meeting the parent's needs. The child already feels emotionally abandoned, and expressing needs raises the fear of more abandonment. Children assign blame to themselves and find it difficult to understand or see that the needs of the parent are self-serving. They feel guilty and obligated, and with no other option, they strive to please. They are trapped.

As the children become adults, this entrapment continues as long as the reality of being a covert incest victim is denied. Adults continue to feel ashamed of their dependency needs and seek to fulfill parents' needs at a cost to their own ability to be intimate. One important ingredient in learning to be intimate is to accept one's own personal dependency needs. The silent seduction, if not faced directly, continues to sabotage the desire to reap the benefits of intimacy and love with another.

The Family System

All families function as a system in which one person's actions affect another and vice versa. Although each member functions independently, that member also affects and is affected by the whole. Salvador Minuchin, in *Families and Family Therapy,* says the family system has a function or purpose of seeking to bring itself back into balance or stability when disrupted. So in the case of a marriage not bonded in a healthy way, the parents' unmet dependency, intimacy, and emotional needs will be met by the rest of the system—the children.

In a covertly incestuous relationship, the parent complains to the child about the difficulties in the marriage. The child becomes the parent's confidante. Loneliness, bitterness, and dissatisfaction with the marriage and sex life are common topics in these discussions. The child feels "icky" about it, but quickly comes to the parent's rescue and begins to serve as the surrogate spouse the system is lacking. Both parents are active participants in this covertly incestuous relationship. One is getting some needs met through the child and the other is relieved at not having to deal with the reality of the unsatisfied partner. Covert incest victims often report that the same-sex parent encouraged them to comfort the opposite-sex parent after a marital fight or in their absence with statements like, "You take care of your mother while I'm gone; I'm counting on you." The child, hoping to get some of his or her own needs met, readily obliges.

Once the boundary between parent and child is crossed in a covertly incestuous relationship, the potential for more victimization exists. For example, if the oldest boy is in a psychological marriage with his mother, he may act out the covert sexualized energy with a younger sister in an overt sexual way. What started out as a spillover of unmet intimate and sexual needs from the marriage to the oldest boy in a covert way, becomes overt incest between siblings. This example clearly demonstrates how one person's behavior in a family affects the family system as a whole.

The family system works to seek balance and tries to correct itself, even in adulthood. As long as the abuse or neglect experienced in childhood remains buried within, we re-create our family in adult relationships. This is an effort to work out and resolve the childhood pain. Yes, the family system continues to affect one's life even when one is no longer living at home and has dismissed childhood as gone and best forgotten.

As Emily put it:

> *I couldn't believe I married a man just like my father . . . at least he felt that way to me. When I married him, he seemed the opposite of my dad, but after a while, we began responding to each other the way it happened with my dad. My husband began treating me like his "princess," the same way my dad did. I couldn't stand it, yet I acted in ways that demanded that kind of treatment from him. It wasn't until I was about to divorce him that my therapist helped me see it wasn't my husband I wanted to divorce, but my past . . . my father.*

The covertly incestuous relationship system continues to affect one's choice of partners, decisions about separation and divorce, sexuality, and all attempts at emotional fulfillment until the truth is faced and resolved. This is not about blaming or accusing parents. It is about assigning responsibility where it belongs: the parent's relationship with the child. Children do not choose this relationship; it is created for them. Even as adults, we do not gain freedom of choice until we see the past clearly and experience our feelings about it. Relationships continue to be dictated by the sense of entrapment experienced as a surrogate partner to one's parent. Assigning responsibility where it rightfully belongs is the first crucial step in gaining access to one's true feelings, needs, and wants.

It is important to understand that parents re-create their own family systems. Most parents are not malicious and are not aware of the effect they have on their children because a part of their own childhood is buried within. Sadly, if one's own childhood is not seen for what it really was, the pain of these incestuous relationships gets passed on from one generation to the next. If parents never recover their own lost childhoods, their grief deepens. They continue to expect their children to be there for them in ways they wished their parents had been. When this expectation goes unmet, parents see their children as ungrateful, unloving, and selfish. The result heightens struggles between adult children and aging parents. Willpower or the right set of moral standards isn't enough to produce lasting, healthy changes. Only by facing one's past can one take responsibility for oneself and reclaim the vitality surrendered by being a parent's surrogate partner.

Let's look at two specific types of family systems that produce a covertly incestuous relationship between a parent and a child—the alcoholic family and the dysfunctional family.

THE ALCOHOLIC FAMILY

Ann is a thirty-six-year-old professional and mother of two children. On the surface she always seemed happy and to have everything going for her. When her marriage began to collapse, she entered therapy and support groups for adult children of alcoholics. Ann described growing up in her alcoholic family.

My mother was the alcoholic in my life. I was the eldest of four children and always had the duties of taking care of my brothers and sisters, the house, and my dad. I resented my mother for this. But my dad praised me so much and gave me so much special attention for being the "little mother" around the house for him, that eventually I didn't seem to mind my mother's alcoholism. My dad would always let me sit in his lap at night for being "his girl," comb my hair, and do special things for me. Something didn't feel right about it, but it was the only attention I got.

As an adult, I seemed to have everything going for me and seemed in control. But my husband confronted me one day and said he was dissatisfied with my difficulties in being intimate with him. He wanted changes or a divorce. I was stunned. That's when I discovered that growing up in an alcoholic family affected my ability to be intimate. I figured if I dealt with my feelings and issues about my mother, things would be fine. After all, she was the alcoholic. Well, I did deal with her, but things weren't fine. I came to realize that all that special attention from my dad was really a source of pain and the real culprit behind my difficulty in being close to my husband.

Now I realize that I've lived my life for him. I chose my husband because I thought my father would approve. The career and family I built were intended to win my father's admiration and love. Even as an adult, I went to him with intimate details of my life, which he invited. God, I began to feel icky all over again. I was scared and guilt-ridden. I knew I had to stop being "Daddy's girl" if I was going to save myself and my marriage. It was the most difficult decision I ever had to make about my life: separating from the man who had been *the only source of comfort while I was growing up. Yet it was also the most freeing decision I ever made.*

There are an estimated 26.8 million children of alcoholic parents in this country, according to the National Association for Children of Alcoholics. Of that group, many have played the role of a parent's partner to fill in for the emotionally or physically absent alcoholic. These are the ones who, as adults, appear to have it all together and organized. They are high achieving, in control, successful, and giving. They are also the ones who struggle intensely with feeling undeserving and incapable of intimacy. This pain and struggle is often hidden behind a mask of competency and proficiency in helping others. These are the children of alcoholic parents who are described as the "heroes" and "responsible" ones.

These are roles that develop in all families during times of stress as the system tries to bring itself back into balance. In the alcoholic family, the children get stuck in the roles unless there is recovery of both the alcoholic and coalcoholic (partner of the alcoholic). Alcoholism is a progressive disease process where the alcoholic becomes more and more attached to the bottle over time. Someone whose attachment is to the bottle cannot be emotionally attached to a partner. The vacancy created by the progressing disease makes room for a surrogate spouse. The hero or responsible child fills that space through no choice of his or her own.

The child is compelled to play the surrogate partner because it is a gratifying source of self-worth in a family with little worth to share. Again, this pattern holds true in adulthood. If the coalcoholic is not in recovery, he invites and seduces a partnership with the child out of desperation to have needs met and to deny the reality of the progressing alcoholism. Alcoholic families are a true breeding ground for covert incest. Many heroes and responsible adult children have been its victims.

Heroes and responsible adult children have benefited from the recovery process offered by adult child support groups and specialized therapy programs. They have been able to let go of some of their perfectionism and feel a sense of belonging, for perhaps the first time in their lives. However, many still suffer in silence over their continued struggles with intimacy. In that silence is the "ickiness" they feel and the struggles they continue to experience with the coalcoholic. Most fear if they talk about it at their support group meetings, they'll be ostracized by the people whose acceptance they have worked so hard to earn. At their meetings, they do what they do best: people-please in order to be accepted. They don't talk about the truth, saying instead only what they know will be accepted. To do otherwise might "rock the boat" at their meetings. Adult children support groups sometimes have their own unspoken rules, which blame the alcoholic for the pain and continue to idealize and revere the coalcoholic for all the sacrifices offered during the adult child's growing-up years. Out of their own desperation to fill personal emptiness, heroes or responsible adult children who have been covert incest victims perpetuate the pain by abiding by the family rule that Claudia Black summarizes in *It Will Never Happen to Me!*—"Don't talk, feel, or trust."

One of the more difficult tasks for heroes or responsible adult children involves removing themselves from the idealized and privileged pedestal they were given by the opposite-sex parent. Sitting on a pedestal represents being loved for what they can provide their parent, not for who they are. In reality, heroes or responsible adult children who suffered covert incest have been emotionally abandoned and sexually violated. Their personhood (feelings and sexuality) has been objectified or used for the purpose of another, leaving them emotionally and sexually scarred. For them, the struggle is not primarily with the alcoholic, but with the coalcoholic.

The characteristics and patterns of the alcoholic family also hold true when a parent is addicted to drugs (including mood- or mind-altering prescription drugs), food, sex, shopping, spending, gambling, or work. Like the alcoholic, the parent is emotionally absent due to the addiction. As a result, the potential for covert incest exists. Other potential situations include a chronically ill parent or a parent who rigidly holds onto rules dictated by a religious or ethnic tradition. The emotional absence in the second case occurs because the parent is more interested in upholding the moral principles of the religion or the rituals and rights of the ethnic background than in considering the needs of individuals. The emotional life of the parent gets lost, ultimately producing a break in the emotional, spiritual, and sexual bond of the partnership.

Covert incest is a possibility in any dysfunctional family where there is a chronic void in the marriage relationship. We've discussed the alcoholic and substance abuse family system; now, let's take a closer look at the dysfunctional family system.

THE DYSFUNCTIONAL FAMILY

Mark, a thirty-four-year-old successful attorney, has had many meaningful relationships over the years. He now finds himself lonely and destitute regarding intimacy. Mark describes his childhood.

I thought I had the perfect parents. I was particularly fond of my mother, because she was always there for me, to comfort me and talk. We talked about everything. Often she talked about my dad. I always felt special around her because she trusted me with personal information. My father was an attorney who loved his work. He seemed more married to his job than to my mother. But he made sure we had everything—the best clothes, the best schools, and whatever we wanted. It was hard to be angry with him. Besides, as a family, we seemed fine. We were invited to all the "right" places and said and did all the "right" things. We had strong ethnic traditions and followed them to the letter. There was never any overt family fighting or feuds. We seemed real close. And I always found some time alone with my mother at our family gatherings. I always felt special after one of our talks.

As Mark began to face the pain of his loneliness and entered therapy, he described his family differently.

I had no idea there were people who talked about feelings and problems directly. I was shocked to realize my family was dysfunctional. But it was true. No one ever talked about problems except when my mother complained about my dad. I never knew that in functional marriages, partners spoke to

*each other about their dissatisfaction. I thought including me
was my mom's way of making me feel special. I had no idea my
mother was seducing me because she was lonely. I also began
to realize my family's insistence in following tradition was an
unspoken rule that said, "See, we are one big happy family,
and don't anyone challenge that by talking about feelings or
problems directly." It was our way not to "rock the boat" and
to hide all concerns. Behind that mask was the loneliness both
my parents and I experienced. Since I had no knowledge as I
grew up that it was okay to talk about feelings and problems, I
never thought to question my mother's close relationship with
me, even though at times it felt funny to be treated so special.*

Mark went on to describe how his family relationships,
particularly the one with his mother, affected his quest for
intimacy.

*I had many romantic, meaningful relationships with
women. At times, I was involved with more than one woman.
It wasn't until I began to question my family, and see the
system for what it was, that I realized I had ended or destroyed
one relationship after another because none of the women
made me feel like my mother did—her "prince" and "knight
in shining armor." If I did feel "special" in a relationship, that
feeling usually didn't last long. Although there seemed to
be many women interested in a "prince" to "save" them, the
high or excitement of acting and being treated like one never
endured. When the infatuation ended, I was faced with the
realities of the person and the demands of real intimacy. So I*

would drop or destroy the relationship in search of the woman who would make me feel special forever. Of course, this never happened, and I became lonelier than I imagined I could be. I was desperate. I never dreamed this was the result of my family system. For me, having this awareness was both enraging and freeing.

Many men and women have grown up in families where there is no alcoholic or chemically dependent parent, yet the struggles for love and intimacy are similar. In fact, many of these families appear to be the ideal or perfect family on the outside. Such an illusion makes it much more difficult to confront the past, find the roots of one's current struggles, and become healthy. These dysfunctional families have been described as codependent. In *Co-Dependency and Family Rules: A Paradoxical Dependency*, Robert Subby and John Friel offer this definition:

> *Co-dependency is a dysfunctional pattern of living and problem solving, which is kept in place by a set of rules within the family system. These rules make healthy growth and change very difficult.*

The rules described by Subby and Friel are:

1. It's not okay to talk about problems.
2. Feelings should not be expressed openly.
3. Communication is best if indirect, with one person acting as messenger between two others (triangulation).

4. Be strong, good, right, perfect. Make us proud.
   (unrealistic expectations)
5. Don't be selfish.
6. Do as I say, not as I do.
7. It is not okay to play or be playful.
8. Don't rock the boat.

Practiced collectively or separately, these rules make it difficult for people to be close or intimate. The desire to share oneself (that is, through feelings, thoughts, preferences, wants, and needs) becomes a frightening endeavor. The family system's mask of perfection and idealism is threatened. With their codes of silence, these families suffer from chronic tension and the anxiety that lurks below the surface. Remarks such as, "You could have cut the tension with a knife," are not uncommon. Family members operating in these systems are usually relieved no one said anything, for fear of what might happen—"I'm sure glad I got out of there before someone said something."

Talking about feelings or problems helps to resolve tension. These families believe, however, that if they don't talk about problems, the tension will go away. Any sort of emotional bonding between family members is impossible as long as these rules are observed.

Like families with a parent who is absent due to alcohol or drug abuse, families operating under codependent rules create the potential for covertly incestuous relationships. Codependent families originate from marriages that operate in a code of silence. Even though there is no obvious break, healthy intimacy and sexuality have no chance to grow. One or both partners feels dissatisfied. Trapped by a set of rules that do not permit the healthy expression of feelings and problems, a parent can easily turn to a child to get needs met. This child lessens the parent's loneliness and helps the parent deny the breakdown inherent in a marriage built on codependent rules. It is easy to see how a parent can channel his or her passion and energy into the child and how that child can feel like the parent's surrogate partner.

For the adult child of a dysfunctional family, the task of seeing the family for what it is becomes difficult due to the family's rigid adherence to the idealistic or perfect image. To name the covert incest that went on is much more difficult. Yet to break the walls of silence and denial is far better than to keep the pain and suffering of being a parent's surrogate partner secret for a lifetime.

3

∽∾∽

The Man of the House

*Early on we experience women as the ones who fill us up,
who comfort and take care of us, without an opportunity in
growing up . . . to feel truly separate from women.*

—Samuel Osherson, *Finding Our Father*

WHEN ED ENTERED THERAPY, he was forlorn with an air
about him that said, "Don't try to help me. I can do it myself."
Serious in expression and rigid in manner, he answered questions
more like a good soldier than someone seeking help. He wasn't sure
why he was in a therapist's office, except he had felt depressed for
too long and couldn't get rid of this feeling. After many sessions,
Ed finally became more comfortable and began to loosen up.

Mom's Little Man

In an almost proud and boastful manner, Ed described his childhood.

I was seven when my dad left the house. I really never knew why, and I don't have a lot of memories before that age. I only knew I was the eldest in a family of eight, and it just seemed like I was the new dad. In fact, I can still remember my mother's words the day after my dad left: "Your father won't be coming back, and you're going to have to help me with the kids." It was a moment of both delight to be Mom's helper and confusion as to what happened to my dad. When I tried to clear up my confusion by asking my mother what happened to Dad, I was usually met with short, angry comments about what a "no good" man my father was. To this day, I still don't understand why he left. What I do know is that the sadness I felt about my dad leaving was quickly replaced by anger, nurtured continually by my mother. I decided early on I was going to show him I could be a better father than he ever was. Although I didn't know it at the time, I was also working on being a better husband than he was—a role my mother always seemed to welcome.

I took on my role dutifully and became more like a drill sergeant than a brother to my brothers and sisters. I made sure they did their homework, cleaned their rooms, and listened to Mom. When they wouldn't listen to me, I'd yell and scream and sometimes hit them. Once, I spanked my younger sister for not washing the dishes. They all hated me, but at the time it didn't seem to matter. Because Mom always supported my disciplining the kids, I felt powerful and deserving. I also began doing odd jobs in the neighborhood and got a paper route so I could help Mom support the family. I was serious and dependable, so I readily got jobs that were meant for someone older. By the time I was eleven, I was handing out allowances to each of my brothers and sisters. In school, I always felt distracted by my responsibilities at home and never had time to play or join extracurricular activities. By the time I was twelve, I was a grown man who had never known the meaning of play and fun.

It is clear Ed had lost his childhood long ago and had become the "man of the house" in a family desperate for structure and direction. His teen years continued the pattern.

More and more, my mother and I stayed up late, talking. I loved our talks. She would tell me about her day and how glad she was I was home waiting for her. Sometimes she cried about how lonely she was and leaned against me on the couch until she fell asleep. I would cover her up and kiss her good night before going to bed myself. There were moments when I wished I could have lain with her. Although those feelings alarmed me, I felt too ashamed to say anything to anyone. Besides, there was no one in my life I could talk to, except my mother.

One Christmas I decided I was going to make my mother feel special so she wouldn't have to feel so lonely. I went out and bought her expensive perfume, a special nightgown, and a fancy necklace. She loved the gifts and seemed to love me more. She held me close while we watched everyone else open their presents. That night she kissed me good night and told me I was her "little man." It felt great being treated so special. It gave me a feeling of power.

It wasn't until I started dating and bringing home girlfriends that I began to feel anger toward my mother. At first it seemed nice to be able to come home and talk to Mom about my dates, but then she began to get jealous. In fact, when I became serious about Susan, my mother forbade me to see her and accused her of being a slut. I stormed out of the house and made my way to Susan's house. By the time I got there, my rage was covered over by a sense of guilt that permeated every cell of my body. To my surprise, I broke off my relationship with Susan and went home like a puppy with its tail between its legs. I was still angry, and I felt trapped.

Finally, when I was twenty-four, I left home to marry Karen. Karen was a nice girl. My mother didn't seem too threatened by her and reluctantly approved of her. It seemed like a juggling act to attempt to get my needs met and not feel guilty at the same time. Shortly after I married, I became engrossed in my work. I was powerful, competent, and successful on the outside, but I felt impotent and angry on the inside. My marriage lacked vitality and passion. I felt as trapped in my marriage as I did in my relationship with my mother, who always made her presence known in my life. At work, I began to find myself more and more angry at female subordinates, eventually being *seen as a chauvinist. At other times, I found myself acting seductively with these women and contemplating affairs.*

When I failed to get a promotion because of my attitude problems at work, my world seemed to fall apart. I became more and more depressed. Inside I was screaming, "Help, this is not who I am!" Yet I had no idea who I was. Guilty, confused, and angry, I finally sought help.

Ed's story is like that of many men who spent their childhoods being "the man of the house." Men like Ed are emotionally unavailable for intimacy. They often hide their pain and suffering behind an arrogant, boastful facade. Men like Ed are lacking an emotionally fulfilled and sensitive identity because of their mothers' repeated violations of their personal boundaries and the abandonment caused by the absence of their fathers.

Due to their shame and confusion, "Mom's little men" bury their rage and hurt through denial. Feelings suppressed in childhood often find their way out through one's personality and defensive behavior patterns in adulthood. These painful and angry feelings from childhood make it difficult to be comfortable with closeness and intimacy as an adult.

The effect of Ed's covert incest can also be seen in his choice of romantic partners. His wife, Karen, had her own difficulties with intimacy. Hiding behind the image of "niceness," Karen was terrified of emotional closeness. Being nice was the only way Karen knew to express her love. Attempts at passion, joy, or healthy conflict were generally suppressed. Ed's marriage to Karen was more his mother's choice than his own. By choosing

Karen, who had her own struggles with intimacy, the marriage was unfulfilling for Ed. It was not a threat to his mother, who remained his primary partner. Karen became the "other woman." Ed's depression resulted from both the long-term grief over a lost childhood and the inability to be engaged emotionally in an adult romantic relationship.

If Ed is to recover his potential for emotional fulfillment and intimacy, he has to face the pain and anger of being his mother's partner. To deal only with the surface issue of attitude problems will not produce any lasting change.

For Ed and Karen's marriage to become fulfilling, Karen will be required to change, too. It was no accident that Karen chose Ed to marry. Karen's own childhood of abuse or neglect would have compelled her to marry someone like Ed. She likely feels compelled to remain on the sidelines of Ed's relationship with his mother to avoid conflict. She will have to learn to assert herself and request changes in the marriage. Once Ed begins to separate from his mother, he will experience the marriage differently as well. He may begin to encounter Karen's own difficulties with being close as he attempts to be fully intimate in the marriage for the first time.

Mama's Boy

Tom entered therapy reluctantly and only because he had become sexually compulsive with prostitutes. He had a history of obsessive masturbation and use of pornography to get high sexually. Recently, however, those methods didn't seem to be working. He vowed he would never visit prostitutes, but found he couldn't stop himself; having sex with prostitutes was taboo and produced the high he was after. He was confused and scared.

When asked to describe his childhood relationship with his mother, Tom offered:

Yeah, I was Mama's boy all right. We were best friends, I suppose. I know I was sure special to her. She took me everywhere with her: shopping, lunch with her friends, and sometimes even to bed with her to sleep when my dad went out of town on business. It seemed she always treated me as her "little baby," even as I grew up. She protected me from my brothers when they tried to start a fight with me. My mom would keep me home from school, even when I wasn't sick. She said she needed some company, and I could make up my schoolwork later. I never did. I was either at home with my mom, out sick, or distracted from my schoolwork because I was worried about Mom. School was a struggle, and I was called names like "sissy" and "baby." My brothers called me names, too, and hated that I was so special to my mom.

Tom continued to describe growing up in his family.

I was the youngest of four children, which seemed to contribute to being "Mama's boy." In looking back, I guess my mother and father never had a very good relationship. My dad was an alcoholic and my mother was very religious. They always bickered. They seldom slept together, and when they did, I was often between them. I was the one who got the good-

morning kiss when we got up, not my dad. Although it seemed a little funny, I liked being treated so special.

My mom pampered me all my life. Anything I wanted, I got. I became oblivious to my brothers and sister and, basically, the world at large. All that seemed to matter was being with my mother. I felt as if my dad hated me. It seemed to me he was actually jealous. Even today, my father mumbles under his breath that it was my fault they got divorced.

I still remember the scene when my mom kicked my dad out. She held me in front of her with her arm around me as she told him she was tired of his drinking and wanted him out. My father yelled back at her that he wouldn't drink so much if she paid half as much attention to him as she did to that "damn kid," pointing at me. He slammed the door. I remember feeling terrified and confused as to why my dad was so angry at me. The next morning he came back, packed his things, and left. It was confusing to me that I didn't even miss him. I didn't know him. My mother had kept me close to her for so long that I didn't know what it was like to have a father.

I didn't date too much in high school, mostly because I felt guilty leaving my mom. I did, however, begin a secret life of masturbating to pictures of women in magazines, and eventually to pornography. I didn't know exactly what was going on, but it relieved me. I started feeling resentful that she wanted me so close. The masturbation seemed to help me deal with my feelings.

I'm not sure what propelled me, but I decided I had to leave the house. So at the age of twenty-five, I left. It was so difficult—my mother was enraged and I felt terrible guilt. I *had to get out. Besides, I had secretly started seeing women. I didn't want to tell my mom, because I didn't think she would understand. I also was masturbating more, to the point where I couldn't live without it.*

I discovered if I played the aimless, cute, little-boy role I learned from my mom, women would "come on" to me. They wanted to take care of me like my mom did. It was an easy way to get sex. I became obsessed with sex and never was able to have a serious or intimate relationship. My mother and I continued to talk often, even though I didn't live with her anymore. She thought it would be a good idea if we spent more time together, so I began to spend some of my weekends with her. I think it was at this point that the compulsive masturbation wasn't enough. Frequently, after a weekend with my mother, I sought sex with prostitutes.

God, I really began to feel confused. Even though I didn't want to admit it, my special relationship with my mom was a source of pain and personal invasion. I began to feel angry with her, but I didn't want to let go of the special attention I was getting. It seemed like I couldn't live without my mother.

Tom's story is one of a sexual addict—someone whose life is unmanageable due to the compulsive pursuit of sexual highs. (There will be a more thorough discussion of sexual addiction in Chapter 5.) Tom's story reflects the escalation in sexual pursuits that are characteristic of sexual addiction. Being sexual with prostitutes represented a violation of his personal value system. The covertly incestuous relationship with his mother was a major factor in his sexual compulsiveness. The fact that the escalation of his addiction began after he went back to spend the weekends with his mother suggests that his rage at being seduced had festered. Being obsessed with sex was the way Tom distracted himself from the pain of the covert incest.

Due to the perceived entrapment from his guilt, Tom found it difficult to accept his rage as legitimate. However, all feelings find their way out, in spite of one's suppression of them. In Tom's case, his sexual addiction was an expression of his rage and shame. His manipulation of women to have sex with them represented an attitude of exploitation of them. His treatment of women as objects to "get" and "use" was the relief valve the rage needed. As his mother's seduction increased, so did Tom's rage.

Also noteworthy in Tom's story was the competition set up between him and his father. The seduction by his mother pitted Tom against his father. Tom's father naturally felt jealous and competitive toward him. This competition is a frequent dynamic in covert incest, with the same-sex parent usually looking like the "bad guy." Tom's father felt pushed out, which may have been part of his mother's unconscious motive. The legitimate anger Tom felt toward his father was due to his father's unwillingness to step in and separate Tom from his mother. Tom's father either perceived the covertly incestuous relationship as too powerful to break into or was relieved by it since it gave him an excuse to leave the relationship with his wife. Some fathers may consciously push their sons into the arms of the mother to escape the marriage, or perhaps act out in an affair. They abandon the son to the mother for their own self-serving needs. In this case, both parents failed to protect their son from the burden that ensued.

Even if the dynamics and feelings are completely understood, therapy is not enough for a sexual addict. Sexual addiction, like all addictions, does not readily respond to advice, logical arguments, insight, or awareness. A recovery process similar to the one used in the treatment of alcoholism is required to stop compulsive sexual behavior. Alcoholics Anonymous is the recovery program used by alcoholics, but there are separate twelve-step programs that exist for sexual addiction. The largest of these communities include Sex Addicts Anonymous, Sexaholics Anonymous, and Sex and Love Addicts Anonymous. (See appendix for contact information.)

The Prince

Handsome, charming, and seemingly able to "talk a good game," Jeffrey began discussing why he wanted to be in therapy.

I was shocked when I discovered through the grapevine at work that because I wasn't married, I didn't get the promotion I was after. I didn't fit the company image. I had worked toward this position for a long time and was counting on it. My qualifications were outstanding. What did my personal life have to do with the job? Initially, I was angry and thought about contacting my attorney. However, after finding myself sobbing at home that evening, I thought better of it. I couldn't remember ever crying before, not even as a kid, except when I wanted my way. I knew something was wrong.

I never questioned my insatiable appetite for the company of women. I never seemed satisfied with dating just one woman. I always had to be involved with many simultaneously. For the most part, I was usually honest about dating around, so I never gave it a second thought. Besides, women seemed more than willing to compete. I loved the attention. It made me feel like a king. Dating became more like a sport than an attempt at developing a relationship. I generally didn't spend more than one or two days in a row with any one woman, thinking I wanted to be careful not to get too tied down. Yet, if I wasn't seeing someone on a given day, I was planning my next encounter. My life became consumed with the pursuit of women. I suspect the reason I didn't get my promotion was more involved than just not being married. I wonder if the reputation I had as a lady's man was what really interfered.

When any woman I was dating began to make demands of my time or wanted a commitment, I stopped seeing her. Shortly after I began looking for a replacement, I usually felt panicky and desperate until I filled the space left by her departure. During those rare times when I had a long-term girlfriend, I felt suffocated and never remained faithful. In my twenties it was, "I'm too young for a commitment." In my thirties it was, "I have some time left." Now, at the age of forty-seven I find myself saying, "I'm not the marrying type." Privately, I've been waiting for the perfect woman. I realize for the first time just how lonely and fearful I really am. It seems I've spent the better part of my life running from something, though I can't see what it is.

Jeffrey had a difficult time relating to a male therapist. Men like Jeffrey usually relate to other men by bragging about their escapades and discussing women the way they discuss the attainment of a sports trophy. Sharing intimately is frightening and avoided at any cost. With women, Jeffrey was likely to brag about himself, embellish stories, and talk "intimately" only as a means to seduce. Relationships with both men and women leave men like Jeffrey feeling alone and empty. Over time, Jeffrey developed enough trust to begin identifying what he was running from.

I never imagined my childhood had much to do with the struggles I was experiencing with women and intimacy. In my family, I was treated like a prince, especially by my mom. I had an older sister who was "my dad's," and I was "my mother's," creating what seemed like a division of loyalty. My mom was always on my side anytime there was conflict. She always indulged me. Anything I wanted, I got. She was at my beck and call. She showered me with gifts, fussed over me, and told me how handsome I was. She would tell me, "Someday, you will be a lady's man."

She was always preoccupied with my appearance and talked about my body. I remember once when I was a teenager she actually made a comment about how good I looked in tight jeans. I felt embarrassed and a little funny but never thought anything of it. Already as a teenager, I seemed to be attractive to girls. It felt great. At school, I got lots of attention from my girlfriends, and at home I got even more from my mom. I see now that even then I couldn't get enough attention from girls.

My mother actually encouraged me to go out with girls, and she never put any restrictions on the time I had to be home. Once I stayed out all night. When I got home in the morning, my mom just gave me a big smile and a kiss, saying she "knew what I was doing." I just smiled back until my father came into the room. He gave me a vicious look and wanted to know where the hell I had been all night. My mother immediately came to my defense and told him I was just being a boy. As she left for work she reminded me, as she frequently did, that I shouldn't get too attached to any one girl so I could "shop around" for the perfect one.

Jeffrey's relationship with his father was strained and distant. His father had given up on trying to win the affection of either his son or his wife. Jeffrey, and his mother's special relationship to him, kept his father out. In time, his father just stayed away and left Jeffrey with his absence.

There was mostly distance between my father and me. He never seemed to have much time for me and spent a great deal of time away from the house. He worked a lot, and sometimes I wondered if he had another woman on the side. My dad never got drunk or physically abused me. He just wasn't there. I never could figure out why my parents stayed together. They were both working professionals and, on the surface, seemed to have no time for each other. But it went deeper than that. Even when they were together, they didn't talk to each other much.

They really were unhappy together. I see now why my mother invested so much energy in me.

The relationship Jeffrey's mother had with him was sexually energized. Jeffrey probably felt stimulated early in childhood by his mother's intense passion toward him. Certainly his tale of his mother's apparent pleasure in knowing he had spent the night with a girl strongly suggests she was vicariously enjoying a fantasy of her own. Confused and with no one to talk to, Jeffrey suppressed his feelings of shame and anger at being violated. Further, he would have had to deny that his mother's treatment of him felt invasive and would have wanted to continue believing he was her "prince." Over time, his feelings of shame and anger buried deeply within evolved into contempt and rage toward all women. Playing the "lady's man" was a mask for his contempt and rage and a way to act out those feelings.

Psychologically, it is generally believed that a "lady's man" or a "womanizer" is really trying to gain control or power over women. In extreme cases, hatred and abuse of women develop. However, at a deeper level, the "lady's man" avoids the pain of being violated by his mother and acts out his rage about her specifically, as opposed to women in general. As time goes on, such a man has to date more, hate more, or abuse more to sustain the denial of feelings about the incest with his mother. In Jeffrey's case, the desperation and panic he felt when he wasn't seeing someone suggest his suppressed feelings were trying to find their way to the surface. Being denied the promotion at work was the catalyst that broke down Jeffrey's defenses and left him with the pain of the trauma of being seduced by his mother and abandoned by his father.

Also at issue here, at least on the surface, is Jeffrey's fear of intimacy. Certainly Jeffrey's inability to make a commitment qualifies him as someone who fears intimacy. Yet just to work at finding ways to help him become more intimate is not the remedy. It is not so much the fear of intimacy that is operating here, but the fear of feelings that a commitment would bring to the surface. A committed relationship would reengage the feelings he has about his mother, and Jeffrey would project those onto the current woman in his life. Fear of engulfment and excessive feelings of guilt and obligation cause the covert incest survivor to remain distant or ambivalent about commitment. With therapy and recovery, a committed relationship can become a healing opportunity. All those feelings and issues, still unresolved, would surface so he could finally work them through. He might finally feel some contentment with love. It's the psyche's way of healing old emotional wounds.

Without the proper context of understanding and the means to alter one's behavior, the pain of the original trauma continues and the old patterns keep repeating themselves. In Jeffrey's case, he seduced and objectified women as his mother did to him in their covertly incestuous relationship. Given the intense passion and sexual preoccupation Jeffrey's mother had toward him, it is possible that she, too, was an incest victim and acted out with Jeffrey what had been done to her. Incest victims may choose partners who have difficulty with sexual boundaries in an effort to work out the shame and anger. Jeffrey's suspicions of his father having extramarital affairs were probably accurate. In turn, Jeffrey's parents were reenacting scenes from their own childhoods. Jeffrey was the next victim in line for the spillover of inappropriate sexual energy transmitted over generations of victims.

One final note regarding Jeffrey's case: He, like many men who have reputations as "womanizers," was primarily interested in the sexual conquest of women. This type of pattern reflects sexual addiction. Jeffrey was able to face this and begin participating in a twelve-step program for sex addicts. As a result, he was finally able to face the feelings he had been running from for years. In time, he developed a sense of hope and contentment.

Mom's Confidant and Advisor

When Peter came for therapy, he complained of feeling burned out and lethargic. He was a successful therapist who, in spite of his thorough understanding of himself, was unable to stop overcommitting and overextending himself. His life consisted primarily of helping, pleasing, and being there for others. He complained of having no sense of identity and no free time for himself. Peter felt unappreciated and taken advantage of. He reluctantly acknowledged that, for some time, he had resented his wife. He complained he was always there to listen to the multitude of problems she had, but he never felt he got equal time. Yet Peter claimed to be going out of his way to be there for his wife even more now than he had done previously. He felt crazy. He was shut down sexually and had lost all interest in being intimate with his wife.

Relieved to have someone listen, Peter talked rapidly and

obsessively, trying to get his whole life story out in one therapy session. His initial focus was his wife.

I first met Susan ten years ago when she was trying to break up with her (then) boyfriend. She was very troubled and needed someone to talk to. I was more than happy to be there for her. I saw it as a way to get her to like me. I knew I could be good to her and could help her change.

Our initial dates basically consisted of me listening and Susan talking about how much her boyfriend had hurt her. I offered support and plenty of advice as to how she should handle the situation. She often showed up crying and confused at my apartment after seeing him. Even our beginnings at being affectionate involved me holding her while she cried about her boyfriend. The first time we made love was after she cried in my arms about him. Privately, I wondered who she was really making love to. It was months before she stopped seeing her boyfriend, and that was only because he insisted they no longer see each other.

Even after that, Susan seemed preoccupied with him. However, I didn't spend much time considering my feelings about the situation, because I was so involved with being her "counselor." Eventually, she seemed to forget him, and we got married. Our marriage continued to consist of me being preoccupied with how she was feeling and adjusting my schedule to meet her needs. I was driven in my efforts to be there for her, believing she would stop wanting me if I weren't helping her in some way.

At first, she seemed to crave the attention as much as I obsessed about giving it. But over time we seemed to grow more distant. Susan no longer seemed to appreciate my efforts to be there for her, and I began to resent her. And my obsession to help only increased. I felt drained and empty. I resented that I wasn't going to be able to count on Susan to be there for me. She also claimed to have lost respect for me because I was always trying to help her. Yet my efforts to manage her life and problems escalated.

I was having similar problems at work. I was unable to set limits on the amount of time I was available for clients and had a difficult time collecting fees. I began to resent the work I loved so much. My friendships were based primarily on me "being there for" or "helping" my friends. I resented that no one seemed to care about my problems. I was so desperate to be liked I never let on to anyone that I had personal problems or personal needs. I did what I knew best to secure friendships: I helped others out. Naturally, I chose as friends those people whose lives were troubled. I have become so resentful I could explode, except I feel too depressed to do so.

Peter's story is not unlike those of other helping professionals: doctors, therapists, pastors, or nurses. On the outside is a mask of competence supported by a proficiency in helping others. Underneath the mask are feelings of neglect, resentment, bitterness, and fear. Needs are met through manipulation of others by always being there for them. These individuals gain their self-esteem through pleasing and helping others. But this sense of esteem is false. Feelings of worthlessness and shame generally prevail underneath the exterior of "being so together." A compulsion and desperation to help others usually consumes the lives of individuals like Peter. They hope that soon they will feel worthy and have their own needs met. This never happens, and the desperation grows.

A closer look at Peter's childhood reveals the origins of the emotional trap in which he finds himself ensnared. Peter was the younger of two children; he had an older sister. His parents were both successful professionals who always presented a good image to those outside the family. However, his parents had chronic problems in their marriage. His father worked a lot, and when he was home he was often moody. Peter's mother was particularly dissatisfied and bitterly complained about her husband to Peter. Peter, the "sensitive one" in the family, was always willing to listen.

I always seemed to be in the middle of the two of them. My mother complained she wasn't getting enough attention and affection from my father. I would tell my dad about it and encourage him to pay more attention to her. He seldom did, and I began to resent him. I then went to my mom to console her. She would go on and on about my father. I would offer advice and counsel my mother so she would feel better.

When I was as young as eight years old, I was telling my mother she didn't have to worry about my dad because she had me and I loved her. I still remember the big smile when I told her "I love you." She hugged me and held me close. It felt so good to be able to make my mom stop crying and put a smile

on her face. I was more than willing to be there for her. I felt
so important and powerful. I continued to tell my father about
how upset Mom was, in hopes that he would change. But he
never did, and I was the one who was there for my mother.

This pattern continued throughout my childhood and
adolescence. After a while, it seemed that my mother actually
preferred my company over my father's. She basically stopped
complaining to him directly about how unhappy she was.
Instead, she talked to me about it. I remember she would call
me into her room after work to talk while she changed clothes.
Although she never actually took off all her clothes in front of
me, she would take off her jewelry and shoes, and unzip before
she asked me to leave. After dinner she would ask me to help
her around the house. She would talk about her day at work
and her problems with my dad. Sometimes it felt funny being
so close to Mom, but it was such a feeling of importance that
it didn't seem to matter.

Even as an adult, I still feel caught between my mom and
dad. I'm the messenger. When Mom is unhappy, she calls me to
complain and then puts Dad on the phone. I can't believe I still
do this. It enrages me, but I feel guilty thinking about setting
limits on my mother. After all, she is the one who cared about
me so much when I was growing up.

Peter's last statement reflects the essence of his adult struggles.
He came to believe his mother's relationship with him was a
statement of her love for him. It may be true that Peter's mother
loved him, but her need to have him around her so much was to

service her own needs, not his. Her behavior was not a statement of love for him but of need for him. As a result, Peter's own needs for love, security, and support were never met. His relationship with his mother became a model or template of how he would seek out love in his adult life. He learned to compulsively abandon and sacrifice himself and dutifully caretake and absorb others' responsibilities and problems as his way of relating. It is not surprising Peter married Susan, a woman who required a great deal of caretaking and was unable to care for him in return.

The covert incest with Peter's mother occurred as a result of the role in which he played the surrogate husband. Counseling his mother about the unhappiness in her marriage was not his responsibility, nor was reassuring her that she was loved. That discussion needed to occur between husband and wife. Sexual energy was certainly felt when he was invited into her room after work. His mother's own neediness prevented her from realizing that her behavior was inappropriate.

Peter's situation did not result in a sexual addiction but rather a sexual shutdown. Denying his sexual expression was a way Peter could remain loyal to his mother. His passion was still his mother's, not his. Circumstances like Peter's could result in sexual addiction or other addictions for that matter—relationship, alcohol, drug, or food. For Peter, work could certainly be considered addictive and a reenactment of the role he played in his family.

Men like Peter are drawn to women they can take care of so as to re-create the role they played with their mothers. The draw is almost magnetic. The hope is, "If I can just be there enough for her, maybe she'll be there for me." Generally, that never happens. Instead, the needs remain unmet and the resentment grows. For the most part, however, the needs Peter longed to have met could not really be fulfilled by his wife. They were needs of childhood, which are more appropriately met through support groups and the therapy process. The emotional bind he was in was a result of his position between his mother and father. That is not to say there weren't legitimate needs that were unmet in Peter's marriage, but his unmet childhood needs overshadowed his marriage, making it difficult for him to find satisfaction with his wife.

Peter's childhood exposure to inappropriate sexual energy also occurred when he acted as a messenger between his mom and dad. As the go-between, Peter was exposed to a passionate energy meant to be exchanged between husband and wife. This was why Peter became so involved with Susan while she was breaking up with her boyfriend. Symbolically, Susan was his mother; her boyfriend was Peter's father. Peter essentially reenacted his unresolved childhood pain through Susan by re-creating what happened to him as a child. Peter's choice of careers in the helping profession and his difficulty setting limits were also a reflection of the bind he was placed in as a child.

For Peter to resolve the issues surrounding his marriage and career, he must address the covert incest with his mother and the abandonment by his father. Trying to resolve his current adult issues by focusing only on the present is like trying to plug a hole in a dam with one finger while other holes keep breaking through. He must address the reservoir of a lifetime of backed-up feelings. Peter needs to resolve his rage, bitterness, and guilt about the role he was placed in during childhood, a role that extended to his adult life. He will have to grieve for his lost childhood and the fact that his needs were not met. This grief is the root cause of his depression.

The Victimizing Process

Peter and the other three men presented in this chapter are not unique. Their stories are common to men who have grown up in alcoholic or dysfunctional families, but covert incest is not limited to the four roles identified in this chapter. Boys playing roles such as the family's or Mom's hero, lover boy, golden boy, or perfect son are also potential victims of covert incest. Identifying this victimizing process is the first step necessary toward getting free of the trap of being a surrogate partner. The covert incest these men suffered has been a source of confusing, progressive rage and shame that has plagued their intimate and sexual lives as adults. Although there are a myriad of issues regarding intimacy for these men, the dynamic of being a covert incest victim is most pervasive.

A few other issues warrant addressing before we move on to stories of women who were their fathers' partners. There is a common reaction among many men when hearing this information about being a covert incest victim: "If it weren't for my mother, nobody would have cared about me. My dad didn't seem to care about me, and I felt abandoned by him. So even though my mom seemed a little overbearing and overprotective, at least she cared about my needs."

First, it is true that these men have been abandoned by their fathers, and this experience is both highly significant and damaging. One's sense of manhood is deeply injured. To capture a vital and healthy sense of being a man requires dealing with the anger and sadness resulting from the abandonment. These men, in adulthood, must also begin replacing the loss that occurred as a result of being abandoned. This process will be discussed more fully in Chapter 7, "Moving Forward."

Second, the reality of being abandoned by the father is clear. It is not confusing, and the feelings are readily accessible if one has the necessary support. However, the reality of a mother's behavior toward a child in a covertly incestuous relationship is not clear. There is a grave distortion in perception. It isn't always the abuse, neglect, or abandonment one suffers as a child that later interferes with happiness, but rather the distortion in perception that results. The classic example of a distortion in perception is, "I beat you for your own good." Certainly being beaten is damaging, but being told it is for one's "own good" is the factor that will haunt the child for a lifetime.

Being a covert incest victim is no different. It is a distortion in perception to believe that the mother's excess attention given in a covertly incestuous relationship saved the child. On the contrary, it robbed the child of the freedom to be autonomous and to feel worthy. Vitality is lost under the insidious, lifelong trap that "I should keep being there for my mother; after all, she was always there for me." Again, it cannot be stressed enough that the mother's preoccupation with the child is not a statement of love for the child, but a statement of dire neediness by the mother.

The child's core needs are rejected, not served. The child feels like an object, not a person. The real needs for love, nurturing, security, and trust are never met. Worse yet, the child is made to believe those needs are met. This is the essence of the damage in a covertly incestuous relationship, along with the trauma of that relationship being bound by inappropriate sexual energy. The reality of covert incest is hard to see clearly, which is why covert incest is so insidious and pervasive in an adult victim's life.

If you are a man and find yourself identifying with covert incest victims, it would be good to keep in mind that the intent here is not to blame your mother but to hold her accountable. Also important to keep in mind is that your mother's behavior was largely unconscious. Even if it had been conscious, her own neediness from her damaged childhood would have prevented her from taking more personal responsibility. To continue to deny the damage the relationship has caused will keep you trapped in the struggle to find contentment with yourself and your partner. Alternately, to focus only on your anger about your father's abandonment keeps the denial alive.

In summary, denying the reality of covert incest and staying a victim is a setup for some form of addictive or compulsive lifestyle. Because of the broken spirit, the pain and discomfort of being objectified during childhood, and feelings of inappropriate sexual energy in the parent-child relationship the adult covert incest victim has a difficult time being comfortable with his body. Addictions represent an escape from the body and a way to medicate feelings. Sexual addiction and workaholism have already been mentioned in some of the stories. However, food addiction, alcoholism, compulsive spending, shopping, gambling, and drug addiction are also common; in fact, the list is endless. One can become addicted to anything. Surrendering or letting go of the addiction is the first order of business in identifying and working through the feelings born of covert incest.

4

∽ᴏᴥᴏ∾

Daddy's Little Girl

When my daddy died, it seemed like I lost the love of my life.
I was so in love with him . . . I can't seem to love anyone like
I loved my daddy.

—Anonymous

FOR WOMEN who have played the role of a surrogate spouse, the issues surrounding covert incest are similar to those of men who have done the same, but they are also different. For example, some women grow up playing the role of "Daddy's love" while also being a surrogate partner for Mom; men rarely have surrogate partnerships with both parents. Women can also play the role of their mother's surrogate husband without the sexual

59

tension that is evident with men and their mothers. In these instances, eating compulsions are more common than sexual problems in adulthood.

In addition, women more frequently experience direct sexual touch (overt incest) by their fathers while simultaneously playing the role of his surrogate spouse. When this occurs, there is a deep injury to a woman's core sense of self. The consequence to her in adulthood is a sense of living on an emotional roller coaster, riding to the top of romantic fantasies, then plunging into the despair of romantic disillusionment. Feelings and reality remain insulated behind illusions of loving and being loved. Her search for love is driven and desperate, and a sense of union with men may never be felt except in the throes of passion. Underneath this longing and struggle for companionship is the pain and anger of her incestuous violation.

Daddy's Special Love

Vickie, a thirty-seven-year-old professional, was attractive, fashionably dressed, poised, and articulate. She had an air of confidence found only among the most competitive. In fact, Vickie's concern upon entering therapy was that while she knew how to attract and be competitive with men, she did not know how to "keep" them.

Men always seem to be adversaries. I'm careful never to let my guard down around them. I often take pride and joy in seducing them sexually, then abandoning them. There is a certain victory in knowing that I'm wanted. I've always entertained the belief that I had a right to act toward men as they do toward women. Using men was a rite of passage for me in becoming successful. Lately, though, I hate myself for engaging in the same behavior I've always despised in men.

Vickie spent her first therapy session examining her self-contempt. Appearing agitated, she shifted the conversation to her most recent relationship.

It seems when I do become interested in somebody, I manage to chase him away. Greg was no exception. Our relationship started out passionately, as all of mine do. There was something about Greg, though, that made me want more. I became consumed with him. When I wasn't with him, I couldn't stop thinking about him. I would think about how he smelled, looked, dressed, what he might be doing at the moment—anything to keep me intoxicated with him. I rarely let my guard down with someone, but when I did, there was no stopping me. It was all or nothing.

I called him constantly and wanted to be with him every minute. He began to feel suffocated and wanted me to back off. I couldn't. His attempts to get some space from me only made me want to be with him more. Soon his withdrawal from me ignited rage. I attacked him and accused him of not caring. Later, when I calmed down and realized what I had done, I would apologize and try to make up by being sexual. That pacified the situation for a time, but eventually, that didn't work either. Greg spent less and less time with me.

And my attitude became more vicious, to the point where I did everything I could to emasculate him. The very man I had fallen so in love with now was the object of my hate. Finally, he had enough, and told me to stay out of his life.

Vickie's scenario with Greg reflected a pattern of relating to men that she had been frozen in for some time. Unable to hide behind her romantic and sexual illusions any more, her broken heart and lost chances for love consumed her. Women like Vickie approach relationships with a high degree of romantic intrigue, which distorts perceptions about the relationship and the man himself. Instead of falling in love with the man, these women fall in love with the romantic fantasy. A spiral of disillusionment, pain, and emptiness follows. Because she is brokenhearted following each lost love, the woman's desperation for romance and sexual excitement increases. It generally takes greater and greater distortion in perception to fit some man—any man—into the next level of romantic illusion.

Vickie went on to describe the pain and emptiness that followed her thwarted attempts at relationships.

God, I feel so depressed. I feel suicidal when relationships don't work out. I was so afraid of what I might do to myself after Greg dumped me that I realized I needed to be in therapy. I don't know why I even bother falling in love. Sometimes I think it would be easier to see men for sex only and keep love out of it. Yet, there seems to be a deep emptiness in me that longs to be filled with love.

I have a hard time admitting my struggles to be close to men. Perhaps even more difficult is admitting that I desire that closeness. I have always hidden behind a mask of professional competency, anger, and competitiveness with men. As unfulfilling as it was, at least I could relate to men in some way.

Vickie's defenses were no longer working. She could not tolerate the pain and hurt of the abused little girl inside her. Vickie's desperate, illusory, and anger-filled attempts at relationships were her unconscious drive to become aware of and resolve the abuse she suffered as a young girl. The extremes in Vickie's behavior toward men are common among women who have been "Daddy's little girl" or "Daddy's love." A closer look at Vickie's relationship to her father reveals what underlies her pain and anger.

When asked to describe her parents, Vickie was quick to start with complaints of her mother.

My mother was always complaining about something. I couldn't stand her. I couldn't do anything right in her eyes; she was always on me about something. Even though I had an older brother and two younger sisters, I always had the feeling she took special pride in criticizing me more than them. She seemed jealous of me, and I couldn't quite understand why. I always felt like I must have done something horrible. I was always left feeling like a bad little girl around her.

I don't have much memory of specific childhood events. In fact, I don't have any memories much before the age of five. After that, my memories are filled with the constant antagonism between my mother and me. Life was a chore at home, knowing I had to face her on a daily basis. My only pleasant memories were of my father. He seemed to love and adore me so much. If it weren't for him, I never would have felt any love growing up. Even though he drank some, and was possibly an alcoholic, at least he had a heart.

I loved and adored my daddy as much as he did me. We had a special relationship. He took me special places and brought home gifts just for me. At night I was the one who got to sit next to him or on his lap. I was always so excited to be around him. When we were alone, he told me how much he loved "his little girl" and if it weren't for me, he would have left my mother long ago. All the while growing up, I knew I could be a better companion to my dad than my mother was. After all, I could tell he preferred me.

My father was a favorite target of my mother's criticism when he wasn't around. She attacked him intensely when I was present, almost as if for my benefit. She complained about his drinking and griped that he spoiled me too much. I would defend him and argue back that I wasn't spoiled. She acted suspicious whenever I spent time alone with my father and asked an endless number of questions. I always felt like I'd done something bad, that I was dirty. Being loved by my daddy had a price. Somehow, I was always left feeling ashamed for receiving the loving attention I got.

When it was suggested that Vickie's relationship with her father was a significant reason for her pain and struggles in relationships, she protested. "I can see that he was the one who loved me, but I get sick to my stomach and frightened thinking about looking at my father's relationship with me."

After months of therapy, Vickie began to let herself in on the pain and violation created by her father's relationship with her. She also began to recall events from her childhood. She reported that throughout her childhood, and sometimes as an adult, she would have what she thought was a dream: "A dark-figured man keeps coming toward my bed, but I can't see his face; the dream always stops there. I always wake terrified and confused."

One day, Vickie came into her therapy session sobbing:

> *I know who that man is. It's my father. I saw him in the dream last night. He was touching me sexually. I can't believe it. It must have happened about age four or five. That was not a dream I was having but a memory. I can see him. I don't want this to be true! But I can smell him like it was happening now. The scent of his cigarettes and booze is right there.*

Vickie began to work through her pain and rage. She attended a women's support group for incest victims and received support for her feelings surrounding the abuse. Her lifetime of buried anger at her father was expressed by her anger at and seduction of men. Her seductive pattern allowed her to feel powerful and to temporarily overcome her childhood feeling of helplessness. Vickie had kept these feelings hidden behind the illusion that her daddy was "all good and loving." Children who are abused often have no choice but to create a false, illusory image of the abusing parent, which enables them to believe they are loved.

Children will hold onto this belief at any cost; their need to believe they are loved is as vital as is their need for food or water. For this reason, many abused children idealize the abusing parent. They often go on to re-create "betrayal bonds" in adulthood, where abuse and love become mixed together in romantic relationships.

After the hurt and pain subsided, Vickie was relieved to have learned the reality of her abuse. However, she struggled with breaking through the illusion created by her father's special attention to her. She was willing to acknowledge she had been a victim of overt sexual abuse, but not of covert incest. After all, her father's special attention to her was the only love she got, and it enabled her to remain on a pedestal above her mother, the parent with whom she felt so competitive.

Once Vickie started to understand her mother's motivations, she saw things more clearly. Vickie's mother was suspicious about the time Vickie spent alone with her father. Vickie often felt anger and blame from her mother but never understood why. She sometimes wondered if her mother faulted her for the abuse. It was easier for Vickie's mother to be angry with her, than confront her husband. Once Vickie began to recognize that she and her mother were competing for the same man's attention, she began to put her mother's anger at her in perspective.

Vickie realized that her father's seduction of her was a method he used to keep his wife's anger at bay. By keeping Vickie seduced in a "close" relationship, he left his wife feeling jealous and competitive. The anger and pain about her husband's abuse became secondary to the importance of competing with her daughter. A competitive, covertly incestuous triangle was cocreated by both parents. As Vickie began to become aware of this through therapy, her childlike illusion of her father's love began to shatter. She saw him for who he really was.

In her adult life, Vickie's emotional roller-coaster ride of romantic fantasy and intrigue followed by painful disillusionment was the consequence of this false image of her father. Her view of all men was filtered through this original distortion. Becoming attached only to the fantasy rather than the reality of the men in her life, Vickie kept her father's seduction hidden from her awareness. She never had to face the painful feelings required to live in reality. After facing the facts and working through her feelings, Vickie began to approach a relationship more realistically and see a man for who he was. The roller-coaster ride was finally coming to an end.

The new stability in Vickie's life was assisted by the recovery from her sex and love addiction. Through her attendance at support groups for this addiction, she realized she had created a pattern in her life that was out of control. In fact, as time went on, Vickie revealed more about her pursuit of sexual highs than she had first acknowledged. Her initial admission of driven romantic and sexual relationships was only part of the story. Vickie's history confirmed a pattern of sex and love addiction.

This description departs somewhat from the identification of sexual addiction that was discussed in Chapter 3. In some cases, describing one's pattern as both sex and love addiction is more accurate. This is more common among women than men. However, many men who identify a sexual addiction are also driven to pursue love at any cost.

The Princess

Although many women are not overtly abused sexually, they can be locked into a sexualized relationship with their fathers. Such was the case with Rebecca. She came into therapy complaining about her husband. This was her third marriage. None of her husbands had ever pleased her, and she had an endless list of complaints about each. The first two husbands left the marriage because they had "had enough of my complaints and dissatisfaction."

Although Rebecca made this statement, she went on to place the blame for the failed marriages on her husbands. She was unable to view her own behavior in context and see how she had affected her husbands. Rebecca's blaming persevered as she proceeded to discuss her third marriage.

> *I seem to have picked yet another man who can't be intimate. Michael is just involved in himself. He never has enough time for me. I need something more. I sometimes think he doesn't even love me because he hardly pays any attention to me. I want to be loved and adored. Michael won't or can't do that. He claims he always makes it a point to set some time aside and connect with me when he gets home from work, but he only does it because I ask him to. I want him to do those things because he loves me. I shouldn't have to ask for what I want or need.*
>
> *Besides, after he makes his perfunctory connection with me, he wants time to himself. He claims to be tired from working all day and wants to relax. I tell him that's my point:*

he never has enough time or energy for me. Sometimes I get so mad I start screaming at him. I let him know if he doesn't start paying more attention to me, we're through. I want him to let me know I'm loved and special in his eyes. The lavish gifts he used to pour on me don't work anymore. I'm special, and I want to be treated that way. I guess I've come into therapy because I really don't want to have to go through another divorce, but Michael is just going to have to do some changing for it to work.

Maybe Michael and I need a long, fun vacation together. Some place new and different. Perhaps I'm just bored. Maybe I don't really know what I want. I can't seem to feel satisfied about my life anymore. I'm starting to feel kind of empty. Maybe if I got pregnant I would be happy. I bet a baby would adore me and love me. Then again, I couldn't do what I wanted when I wanted to. Having a baby might be too inconvenient. I know Michael wouldn't help out. Even if he did, he would have that much less time and energy for me. I'm confused. I want to feel special inside again.

Rebecca's delivery in describing her dissatisfaction was passionate and full of conviction. Though there was probably some truth to the fact that Rebecca chose men who had difficulties with intimacy, the truly relevant issue was her own intimacy struggles. As I continued to listen to Rebecca's complaints, it became apparent to me there was nothing her husband could have done to please her. Her dissatisfaction wasn't really about him, it was about her own inner emptiness and longing for love that occurred well before she met Michael. Her desperation was evident when she switched back and forth between whether Michael or a baby or both could finally fulfill her.

However, Rebecca could not see this reality. She was convinced Michael needed to do something different so she could feel happy again. The inability to see her behavior in a more realistic context and to separate her own issues from those of the relationship was a consequence of an early childhood trauma. The trauma was due to never being seen as a separate person with different needs, wants, preferences, and feelings by one or both of her parents. The consequence of this in adulthood was a narcissistic reality. Rebecca could only see the reflection of herself in Michael. The fact that she became indignant because Michael wanted some time to himself after a long day's work was a reflection of her narcissism. Her insistence that he was taking time away from her reflected Rebecca's struggle in seeing that Michael could have needs or wants separate from her own.

The fact that Rebecca imagined that having a baby might answer her need to be loved revealed her narcissism, too. She would likely be unable to see her baby as having independent needs as well. Rebecca's injury is great. Her defense is to externalize—believing a vacation, a baby, or an adoring husband will take away the pain of never having been loved and seen for who she really is.

After many months of therapy, Rebecca stopped focusing externally on her husband as the cause of her unhappiness. She slowly began to realize that her inner emptiness came from being seduced and abandoned as a little girl.

Rebecca had been her family's princess. On the outside,

she seemed to have it all. She was indulged by her parents and seldom held accountable for any misbehavior. Rebecca frequently received special privileges and rarely wanted for anything. Her siblings hated her, and her friends were envious. It is difficult to imagine that a child treated in such a special manner could have been so deeply injured. She was adored by her father. As she described the specialness she felt from her father, the emotional damage she endured became clearer. Rebecca's father treated her more like his mistress than his daughter.

As Rebecca began to recount her father's relationship to her, the "ickiness" of his seduction became evident to her. Though she had never been sexually touched by him, Rebecca squirmed in her seat as if to get her father off her. She grimaced and exclaimed,

> My dad actually bought me sexy underwear. I can't believe it! I forgot all about that. It felt a little funny at the time, but he always said I was his "princess" and deserved the best. So I didn't think much more of it. Besides, I liked being treated so special. When I started developing breasts, my dad would look at me with a big smile and proclaim, "You are becoming a woman." At that point he started taking me out shopping and buying me whatever I wanted. I'd come out of the dressing room with my new clothes on to get his approval. That felt funny, too, but I didn't think much about it since I really loved being treated so special.
>
> I've always been my dad's favorite. He paid lots of attention to me at home and wanted to know all about my day. He adored me, and I knew it. I began to expect that from everyone in my life, especially men. He even talked about boys to me,

telling me I should find a man who would love me like he did.

Even as an adult, he continues to adore me. I almost seem more special to him than my mother. Last week, when I was at their house, my dad wanted to go into the family pool for a swim, just the two of us. It felt kind of icky, but he said he just wanted some time alone with "his doll." That night, when I got back home, I binged on food. The next morning I starved myself and exercised until I pulled a muscle. Throughout my life, overeating has been an off-and-on pattern. Sometimes I used to vomit or take laxatives as a way not to become overweight. I've stopped that, but now I'm into compulsive exercising and dieting.

Rebecca's struggles with an eating disorder were another consequence of the sexually charged relationship her father had with her. Although she suppressed the memory of her father's seduction, her body continued to carry the feelings and sensations of this trauma. Her eating disorder masked her body's attempt to bring to consciousness the awareness of the sexual injury. The preoccupation with food and weight helped keep the reality hidden. Compulsive overeating, binging and purging oneself (vomiting, exercising, or taking laxatives), or starving oneself are eating disorder patterns common to victims of both covert and overt incest. The energy spent focused on food and weight leaves no room for the body to heal. As Rebecca began to validate her inner reality of being a covert incest victim, the compulsion to overeat slowly subsided. She also took advantage of the support of Overeaters Anonymous to help her overcome her compulsion.

It was crucial that Rebecca directly address both the compulsive-eating pattern and the root cause of the compulsion. This is contrary to an unwritten rule expressed from time to time by members of twelve-step programs: Understanding the reason behind the addiction is not important. One is sometimes encouraged to use the support and philosophy of the twelve-step program and forget the "why." Though there is some merit to this belief in the early part of recovery (stopping the compulsive behavior and making one's life more manageable), it is actually a hindrance to ongoing recovery (peace of mind, comfortableness with one's own body and self, and emotionally fulfilled and functional relationships with others). In my experience, those people who give in regularly to their addiction (be it food, sex, gambling, or other addictions) are the ones who remain in denial about the root injury that opened the way to the addiction in the first place.

The preoccupied relationship Rebecca's father bestowed upon her was motivated by his needs, not hers. Rebecca was seduced into a sexualized, idealized relationship with her father, believing his special attention was all she needed. Simultaneously, she felt emotionally abandoned. Her legitimate needs for love, belonging, and separateness were never met. Being adored and admired were her only clues to the mystery of what it would finally take to fill up the restless, empty space that lay in her soul.

Rebecca's narcissistic reality was her prison. By continuing to complain that Michael wasn't paying enough attention to her, Rebecca hoped to recapture the specialness she once felt as "Daddy's princess." Yet it was this very focus that kept her from realizing the true emotional injury that resulted from being treated in such a special way. No one was ever going to be good enough for Rebecca. She was still in love with her daddy. As Rebecca faced the reality of her father's relationship to her, her emotional freedom began. Her experience of grieving the emotional losses she endured as a little girl finally allowed her to accept the fact of her father's seduction. The true reality of her childhood was the key for which she had been searching. Her heart finally started to heal.

The narcissistic reality present in Rebecca's story is a common consequence of being a covert incest victim. These victims demand more than their fair share of attention and often require being the center of attention, even at the cost of another's feelings. While they typically do not intend to hurt others, they generally lack the empathy needed to know that other people are being affected by them. They are thin-skinned, and defensive if confronted. They can dish it out, but they can't take it. This is, of course, true for both men and women. Since the covert incest victim is never really seen by the parent as uniquely separate, she in turn has difficulty acknowledging the fact that significant others in her life have needs of their own. To varying degrees, covert incest victims essentially see the world revolving around them. Correcting the distorted perceptions inherent in such a reality is a major issue for all covert incest victims. (See bibliography for books on narcissism.)

It bears mentioning that Rebecca's father was probably sexually obsessed and addicted. He violated significant boundaries with his daughter. This suggests his inner reality was lost to sexual intoxication. Many parents may notice their child's attractiveness. That in itself is not damaging. It is in the sexualizing of the child that the violation occurs.

Rebecca's parents had chronic difficulty in their marriage. Both participated in making Rebecca the princess. By participating in keeping Rebecca her father's princess, her mother did not have to deal directly with the problems in her marriage. Both of Rebecca's parents used the sexualized relationship between father and daughter to avoid dealing with the dissatisfying expression of intimacy and sexuality in their marriage.

Father's Love and Mother's Surrogate Husband

For women who experience covert incest as children, playing the role of a surrogate spouse to *both* parents is devastating, perhaps the most tormenting of the situations presented so far. The result is a loss of clear identity. One's inner life feels empty and agonizing. Awareness of feelings, choices, preferences, wants, and desires is lost under a deep sense of unworthiness and inadequacy. Outwardly, these women seem to be able to do it all. They also are capable emotional caretakers of others. They leave the impression that they have few cares of their own, and if they do, they handle them just fine. Yet there is great pain in the experience of self for these women. They struggle with their own sense of femininity and feel conflicted and guilty when attempting a relationship with a man.

In an alcoholic or dysfunctional family, it is often the eldest daughter who occupies this dual role. However, it is not limited to the oldest. Any number of circumstances can change that. The middle daughter could be both parents' favorite and be seduced into a covertly incestuous relationship with them. Or it could be the youngest daughter who is trapped by the dysfunction found in her alcoholic family.

Family dysfunction is progressive. It never stays the same. As it progresses, appropriate boundaries between parent and child may become nonexistent and communication between parents becomes increasingly strained. If an older daughter isn't already a surrogate spouse (or has left the home), the youngest has no choice but to pick up the slack. Often the departure of an older sibling leaves younger siblings vulnerable to covert incest. This does not mean that the incestuous bond between the oldest sibling and parent is severed, but that there are now more players in the drama.

Sue happened to be the oldest daughter in an alcoholic family. She came to see me because of ongoing difficulty in her current relationship. Sue immediately took command of the therapy session by offering a concise description of her family. It seemed so well thought-out, I guessed Sue had more to hide than reveal. She described her family dysfunction in a way that suggested she had handled it well and put it all behind her.

My dad was the alcoholic. He wasn't a bad drunk, but he did drink a lot. Sometimes he would get wild with rage, screaming and yelling at me or my mother. I was afraid of him at those times and stayed away. When his attacks were over, he was always sorrowful. He looked like such a little boy that I would try to comfort him. It was hard to stay mad at him.

Though I was afraid of him at times, I knew I was special

to him. His nickname for me was "Daddy's love." He would frequently let me stay up late with him after everyone, including my mother, had gone to bed. I would sit on his lap with my arms around him while he talked about his day. He talked of my mother frequently. He talked about how unhappy he was with her, and that he wasn't sure why he married her. He used to tell me I must have been the reason he married my mother. He often added that he thought I was the only reason he stayed married.

After our talks at night, my dad would put me to bed. This was my favorite part of the evening. He would lie down next to me and hold me. Sometimes he told me stories or just how much he loved me. I loved it when he fell asleep with me. When I awoke in the morning, he was always gone. At times I felt like I had done something wrong because he didn't stay. I really felt ashamed. When he stopped putting me to bed, I felt I'd done something to cause it—I'll never forget it. One night when I was about eleven or twelve years old, he kissed me on the cheek and sent me off to bed without our special time together. From that point on, there was never any special attention from him at bedtime. No explanations were ever given. I thought for sure I must have done something wrong. Even to this day, I'm still not sure what happened.

Sue sounded more like someone confused by a lover's departure than a woman trying to piece together the fragments of a father-daughter relationship. Even though he may not have had overt sexual feelings for his daughter, falling asleep as frequently as he did with her at night crossed a boundary. Daughters need to have their feelings of "being in love with Daddy" kept within comfortable boundaries—neither too distant nor too close—so as not to feel like the lover. When this boundary is crossed, it is difficult for a woman to share loving, close feelings with a partner of her choice. In covert incest, a daughter feels attached to her father in inappropriate ways. In Sue's case, she also felt rejected, leaving her with even more of a burden. It is probable that at eleven or twelve years of age, Sue began to develop and mature as a woman. Her father might have feared his own feelings and become aware his behavior was inappropriate. Without an explanation, Sue was left feeling at fault for the abrupt change. This gave her a deep sense of shame about her sexuality and growing womanhood.

Throughout her teen years and adulthood, Sue and her father remained special to each other. Though there was no more bedtime closeness, the two continued to have long talks together. Sue's father was the parent she turned to for love and support. She knew he loved her. She was less certain about her mother, though they were close as well.

At night I was very close to my dad. By day it was a different story. I was my mother's best friend; at times I seemed to be her surrogate partner. I provided emotional support and comfort when my mother was feeling depressed, which happened often. If I thought she was sad, I made her breakfast in the morning after my dad left for work. I would tell her not to worry, and that I loved her very much and everything would be all right. She talked a lot about her problems, primarily about my dad.

Even though I felt that my dad and I had a special relationship, it was hard not to side with my mother, too. She seemed so lonely and unhappy. It was hard not to want to comfort and console her, though I hated to at times. I resented the fact that I was her sounding board.

My mother didn't show me the kind of love my dad did. But she always needed me, and I figured she must have loved me. Sometimes at night, we went out together to a movie or dinner and left my dad at home. She said he didn't want to do those kinds of things. I felt torn between them. It was hard to know who to side with. I felt important to both of them. I felt particularly uneasy when my mother complained that my dad *didn't want to have sex with her or couldn't have sex with her; I don't remember what the exact words were. I do remember when they fought, it was a common topic. I think my dad had some sort of sexual problem. I felt terribly guilty, like I was somehow at fault.*

Sue appears to have felt like the "other woman" as a little girl, interfering with her parents' sex life. This only added to her sense of shame regarding her own sexuality. Though the relationship with her father was more sexually charged, the relationship between Sue and her mother had the makings of a similar sexually charged exchange. Sue was made to feel she was replacing her father. The sexual energy was transmitted through the emotional caretaking between Sue and her mother. By having to console her mother, particularly when she complained about sexual matters, Sue likely felt as if she had betrayed her father.

Relatively speaking, Sue idealized her father most and had more difficulty with her mother, but she was still "loyal" to both parents. This more subtle loyalty to *both* parents in a covert incest situation is not as apparent in the previous stories in this book where the split in loyalty is strong and obvious. As dysfunctional as it is, having obvious split loyalties provides some refuge for the covert incest victim. Seeing one parent as all bad, and knowing she is loved by the parent she sees as all good provides a channel for her feelings. Taking the side of one parent allows some sense of relief from the anger and rage. But this was not an option for Sue. As a surrogate partner to *both* parents, she felt at war within herself. Her inner core—her sexuality—was the battlefield.

This inner battle is apparent in Sue's description of her relationships with men.

> *It seems like in one relationship after another, there is some problem with sex between us. I feel as if the men I draw into my life are either preoccupied with sex or somehow feel uncomfortable with themselves sexually. The last man I was involved with, John, was initially charming, although he didn't express a lot of passion. In fact, he seemed void of it, and I didn't feel a lot of passion toward him either. I felt sorry for him. It was almost as if my attraction toward him was based on pity. Even the times we were sexual, it was more obligatory than exciting. Finally, the relationship sort of just dissolved, without any major fighting. I felt relieved. I had begun to feel guilty and burdened, believing somehow I was at fault for John's sexual difficulties.*

The re-creation of Sue's relationship with her mother is apparent in the relationship with John. She confuses love with pity and has a sexual relationship based on guilt and obligation. These are the rudiments of the surrogate partnership with her mother. Sue's attraction to men with sexual difficulties is her attempt to reenact the relationship with her mother and finally separate from her. Though there was never any overt or apparent sexual expression from her mother, Sue's pattern clearly expresses that the relationship was damaging at some level.

Sue went on to describe her current relationship.

Dave is the total opposite of John. He is the other extreme. He is very passionate—too passionate, really. It seems like this is a pattern; first I find a dispassionate relationship, followed by a highly passionate one. Dave seems obsessed with sex. I do things with him that I would never think of doing on my own initiative. Though I feel uncomfortable with some of our sexual behavior, I go along with it anyway, because I know he loves me a lot. After all, he always wants me. Dave has a high sex drive. We make love every evening before we go to bed, no matter how I feel. This is our special time together. Even when we are done being sexual, he often masturbates himself. I feel like somehow I don't satisfy him, even though I am willing to do anything he wants. Recently, we've been watching pornographic movies together. This brought me a lot of shame and was the catalyst in helping me seek therapy.

Sue's relationship with Dave is the re-creation of the seductive relationship with her father. This is the other side of the battle she was caught in as a young girl. Regardless of her father's intentions, his affectionate behavior toward Sue was perceived by her as sexually charged. One of the consequences for Sue in adulthood is to regard exclusively sexual behavior by a partner as a sign of love or affection. This trap invites men who are sexually addicted into the lives of women like Sue.

Sue is a cosexual addict—a person who has a pattern of attracting sexually addicted partners and violating her own value system to please the partner. Thus the coaddict confuses the signs of affection and longs for love so deeply that she accepts sex when she really longs for love. One of the key distinctions between the addict and coaddict is in the belief system, a system addressed by Patrick Carnes in his book *Out of the Shadows: Understanding Sexual Addiction.* Addicts believe sex is their most important need, and coaddicts believe that sex is the most important sign of love. Sue, who felt tremendous guilt and shame about her sexuality, violated her own value system in hopes of satisfying Dave. She hoped to feel loved and special again, as she had with her father at bedtime. Certainly the compulsion to be sexual nightly, regardless of how she felt, was Sue's attempt to recapture what that eleven-year-old little girl lost. But she never received what she longed for. She wanted to be loved as that little girl deserved to be loved—for who she was, not for the comfort she provided her father. Pleasing Dave sexually was never going to fill her void.

In addition to therapy, Sue joined a support group for men and women involved with sexual addicts. (See appendix for a listing of these groups, and the bibliography for more resources on cosexual addiction.) In the beginning, Sue focused on Dave as the cause of her shame and the feelings of humiliation she experienced. Coaddicts commonly have tremendous feelings of betrayal and violation when impacted by their partner's sex addiction. In the beginning stages of healing it is important to allow these feelings to surface and to find ways to establish emotional safety again. It is also critical to look at how coaddiction reenacts childhood issues, where caretaking others needs and sacrificing one's self was a way to have an identity. Coaddiction is a compulsive pattern where there is an external focus on another (typically one's spouse) as either the cause or the cure of feelings of incompleteness and unworthiness.

Sue projected her own unresolved childhood trauma and sexual shame onto the men with whom she became involved. It wasn't until Sue focused on what happened to her as a child rather than as an adult that she finally began to break the bond of addictive relationships.

Coaddicts who remain exclusively focused on blaming others for their relationship struggles merely re-create the situation. Only the names and faces will be different. Sue's life clearly reflects that her relationships were a pattern that could only be broken by looking internally. She had to acknowledge her anger, rage, shame, and guilt about both her parents. Over time, her sexuality stopped being the battlefield for a war that should never have been hers.

Cosexual addiction doesn't have its origin only in a background like Sue's. It can occur with any of the stories presented so far. It seems more women than men become cosexual addicts and more men than women become sexual addicts, although the reverse can also occur. What is clear thus far is that covert incest affects sexuality for both men and women.

5

⌘

When Sex Becomes a Hiding Place

*At the center of every addiction, as at the center of every
cyclone, is a vacuum, a still point of emptiness that generates
circles of frantic movement at its periphery.*

—Peter Trachtenburg

SEXUAL ADDICTION is a misguided attempt at separation
and definition of self for a covert incest victim. It becomes a
perceived gateway to feel separate from the opposite-sex parent
and experience an autonomous sense of self. Not all victims of
covert incest become sexual addicts, nor are all sexual addicts
covert incest victims. Nonetheless, sexual addicts often played
the role of a parent's surrogate partner in their own childhoods.

The entrapment inherent in this covertly incestuous relationship leads to a pattern of addictive pursuits of sexual and romantic highs. These highs offer the covert incest victim an escape. The temporary escape creates an illusion of freedom, which helps fuel the intensity of sexual pursuits.

Sexual addiction is a compulsive drive to act on one's erotic feelings as the only solution to the entrapment inherent in being a covert incest victim. Sexual addiction feeds on itself, with each sexual act leaving a hunger for more. For the addict seduced by the illusion that sex will fill the emptiness of a lost childhood or offer an escape, the most natural of all human desires becomes a source of desperation and its own entrapment.

In its extreme, sexual addiction is life-threatening. Pursuit of new sexual highs becomes the primary purpose in life, although the experience of feeling alive progressively erodes. One is imprisoned by one's own desires. Each attempt at sexual pleasure brings hope for freedom. As the search continues and the risks increase, hopelessness grows. Locked away, the spirit withers and dies. Such is the plight of the compulsive masturbator who risks autoerotic asphyxiation, the womanizer who wakes up next to his best friend's wife only to consider suicide as an option, or the seducer whose string of one-night stands leaves her the victim of a deadly attack by a man she barely knows.

The addiction need not be at these extremes to cause deep suffering. Early on, the addict regards excessive sexual appetite as a way to self-definition. Soon, sexual activity becomes a hiding place rather than a source of genuine love and intimacy. Sexual addiction insidiously depletes self-worth, integrity, and hope. In the wake of its destruction lie despair, confusion, anger, guilt, and shame. Addicts are emotionally unavailable to themselves and to those around them. Relationships with significant others are distant and strained. Work, the one place addicts usually seek refuge, eventually becomes disrupted as well.

Sexual addiction has many forms and does not discriminate based on gender, sexual orientation, race, class, or occupation. It can be as natural and seemingly benign as masturbation or sex within a marriage. Or it can be as damaging and victimizing as incest or rape. Not all rape and incest are committed by an out-of-control sexual addict, yet some sexual addicts commit incest or rape. Conversely, not everyone who masturbates, has an affair, engages in one-night stands, or uses sex to avoid conflict is a sexual addict. However, sexual addicts can and do engage in some or all of these behaviors. A sexual addict can become a prisoner to masturbation, pornography, multiple relationships, anonymous sex, affairs, prostitution, cross-dressing, voyeurism, and exhibitionism. (See bibliography for books on sexual addiction.)

The public is more than willing to label the incest perpetrator, voyeur, or exhibitionist as perverted and sick. The prostitution or pornography junkie is condemned as weak-willed or amoral. But patterns of affairs, multiple relationships, and sexual conquests may not raise an eyebrow or be equally condemned. In fact, they are often normalized and romanticized; yet many of the normalized and romanticized sexual behaviors in our culture have the hallmarks of sexual addiction. These include:

- Secrecy
- Sexual obsession (for example, a constant fantasy-filled stream of consciousness)
- Ritualistic behavior (for example, a certain style of dress) used to enhance sexual excitement or conquest
- Sexual behavior used to avoid reality and feelings (or used to create feelings when there is an absence of feelings in day-to-day living)
- Tolerance to original stimuli with need of increased risks or stimuli to achieve the previous level of sexual excitement (In some cases, tolerance may not occur and the addict may have a stable baseline of addictive behavior.)

Tolerance does explain an escalating pattern of sexual addiction. Tolerance occurs in either fantasy or behavior. For example, an addict using benign fantasies to become sexually aroused may progress to needing sadomasochistic fantasies. Or the addict may switch from fantasies to behavior when the addict reaches a level of tolerance to fantasies alone. The adulterous spouse, for whom sex with a partner across town no longer gives the kind of risk and excitement it once did, might bring it closer to home by becoming involved with a good friend's spouse. When the excitement of the risk wanes, the addict may become careless in keeping the affair a secret. Examples are endless, but all share a common thread of tolerance that drives addicts to violate values, convictions, and promises. The end result is one of destruction and pain for both addicts and their loved ones.

Sexual addiction offers the covert incest victim a sense

of freedom from the weight of the guilt and lack of freedom inherent in the caretaking role of being a surrogate spouse. They are burdened with a sense of never doing or being enough, and are removed from the real or true inner life of who they are. They realize early on that their only source of self-worth rests in sacrificing their own needs and feelings to the emotionally vacant and seductive parent. For a child, there was no choice—it was a matter of survival. Not surprisingly, anger and rage toward the parent festers. Occasionally, when the anger grows beyond tolerable levels and the ego boundaries collapse under the strain, the sexual addict may become victimizing.

When Ray was charged with date rape, his neighbors were shocked. The newspaper article about Ray included a comment by a disbelieving neighbor: "I've known Ray and his mother for a long time. I can't believe this. Ray has always been a good boy. He lives with his mother and takes good care of her. He is always by her side. They must have the wrong man."

Perhaps Ray's relationship with his mother was *too* close. The more seductive, entrapping, and violating a mother's relationship with her son, the more likely that son will displace anger meant for his mother onto other women. The more a man feels unable to separate from a covertly incestuous relationship with his mother, the more likely his sexual behavior will become addictive and victimizing. Such was the case with Ray.

The remainder of this chapter takes a look at the lives of three sexual addicts whose stories are less extreme than Ray's. However, they clearly highlight the role of a parent's seduction in developing the pattern of sexual addiction. Further, the stories demonstrate how covert incest contributes to the double or "split" secret life of sexual addicts. These men and women often hide behind a public life of success and high achievement; they appear to have it so together on the outside, yet they actually have a secret sexual life. The following stories describe a politician, a minister, and a corporate businesswoman.

Will, Age Forty-Seven, Politician

Will was a man who had it all—at least it appeared that way on the surface. His political career was taking shape. His hard work in state and local politics was paying off. His campaigning had led to national office and the likelihood of reelection. He had a successful, growing career, a warm and loving wife, and three wonderful children.

To friends and family who knew his childhood, Will seemed a miracle. Although he came from a successful upper-middle-class family, his growing-up years had been filled with strife and neglect. Among the family Will's father was known to "like his bottle and his women," and his mother was seen as bitter but forgiving. Will vowed early on never to be like his father and quickly filled his father's shoes by being at his mother's side. Family members often commented on the way he was always the "politician" of the family, and how strong he was because he weathered his parents' troubled marriage so well. Will's career, wife, and children were proof he had survived the hidden inner struggles of his early family life. In fact, friends and family privately commented, "He has risen above it."

Then one morning when Will picked up the paper, the headlines and a front-page photo were about him and his lover. Will was filled with rage and shame. He had been involved for months in an affair with a woman he'd met at a political function. Will thought he had kept it secret enough so he wouldn't get caught. After all, his wife, Mary, said she would divorce him if he had another affair. This was not Will's first affair, and he had a reputation as a womanizer and a flirt. As he sat and stared at the paper, Will couldn't believe he had been photographed with his girlfriend in front of his apartment in Washington, D.C. He had forgotten that visit; taking a woman to his apartment was something he always avoided with his new and previous girlfriends. Stunned, he didn't understand why he had taken that risk. *Maybe I wanted to get caught*, he thought.

Will's disbelief and questioning quickly turned to anger and blame. Someone was trying to ruin his career. Besides, he figured he wouldn't have to become involved in affairs if he and Mary were more compatible. Will frequently accused Mary of not being sexual enough. It was his reason for becoming involved with other women. The morning his latest affair was revealed was no different. After briefly expressing remorse and shame, Will launched into a tirade of blame, then pleaded for her forgiveness. Although Mary had heard it all before, she couldn't separate herself from her husband's accusations. As she always did, she believed his blaming and felt sorry for him. Mary wanted to demand that he leave, but her own shame paralyzed her and left her unable to act in her own best interests. Instead, she agreed to play the role of the dutiful wife at her husband's side the following day when he would have to explain himself to the press. This cycle of shame, blame, and minimization is common to sexual addiction.

As the press fired questions, Will denied the affair and Mary claimed he was a faithful husband. As the days passed, however, more evidence surfaced, including an admission by Will's lover. Since the truth could no longer be denied, Will attempted to minimize its significance. But the damage was done. Will's political career was over.

Tolerance and progression help explain why Will risked bringing his lover to his apartment, where he must have been aware he could be watched. It wasn't so much that he wanted to get caught, as he initially believed (addicts try to cover up and hide their behavior, not reveal it), but the insatiable appetite of the addiction drove him to seek riskier situations to increase the high of the experience. Sexual addicts are addicted to the mood alteration that the high offers, rather than the actual sexual behavior itself. The need to feed the addiction interferes with any conscious awareness of the consequences of the action. When consequences surface, the addict uses a mechanism of denial to circumvent the awareness. It might not be far-fetched, for example, to imagine Will thinking, *I won't get caught. I've got my tracks covered*, and *What my wife doesn't know won't hurt her anyway*.

For years, Will kept his affairs, one-night stands, and visits to old girlfriends a secret. Mary knew of some of them and suspected others. Friends and coworkers knew Will strayed from time to time. Before marriage, he had a reputation for womanizing and was regarded as a Casanova. He believed his major identity and purpose was to be a womanizer. At some remote, unconscious level, marriage represented a chance for Will to end this boastful yet painful identity. Much to his surprise, marriage did not curtail his sexual pursuits. Instead, it caused him to keep secret what he had at one time held out as a badge of pride and manhood.

Paradoxically, Will's sense of manhood was inseparably tied to the experience of being romantically and sexually connected to women. He desperately needed the admiration, attention, and company of women to feel adequate. Without them, he felt like a little boy. In fact, Will still was a little boy in the sense that he never emotionally separated from his mother. His romantic and sexual encounters offered him a brief freedom from his mother's grasp and a chance to experience passage into manhood. Will described his childhood.

> *I never received the support I needed from either parent. My mother's relationship with me kept me trapped. My father was never around; he was always drinking or chasing women. I felt I had no choice but to please my mother so she wouldn't leave me. The opportunity to be close to my father was never there. I was my mother's hero and golden boy. Even today, I still feel I'm trying to be her hero.*

In the relationship with his mother, Will learned early on that his self-worth resulted from pleasing others, sacrificing his own needs, and creating a public image of hero or savior. A life of politics was a natural place for Will to act out this role. It was a way to please his mother, feel good enough about himself, and make the statement, "I am a much better man than my father."

Covert-incest victims look to places and circumstances in life where they can overachieve and attempt perfectionism. But they never feel adequate. They are ridden with guilt that they haven't done enough, shame that they "aren't enough," and anger that their needs are not met. The sexual arena offers a place to get a quick fix and be relieved of the burden of the covertly incestuous trap. Sexual acting out allows the covert incest survivor to feel temporarily free from the need to please others as a way to feel loved and valued. But as the strive for perfection grows, the hunger for adequacy and conquest in sexual encounters escalates. A double life is created, and one begins to feed the other. As the shame of the sexual addiction increases, the striving to accomplish increases as well. This increases the very guilt, shame, and rage that drive the addiction. It's a vicious cycle that feeds on the illusion of freedom and power that the double life creates.

Will's political career was over. He had lost the respect of his wife, friends, and family. Yet, his mother continued to defend her "wonderful son." Most important, Will lost respect for himself. He spent many days trying to bolster his damaged esteem by proclaiming, "I will make a comeback." He even gave a public apology in the hope of diminishing the public's mistrust. He vowed to himself and to his wife this would never happen again; he had learned his lesson.

The true extent of the damage from his behavior was not yet realized. Will's relationship with his wife and family was tense, shame-filled, and combative. "Life at home was miserable, and I still blamed Mary," he admitted. "When I realized a political comeback would never happen, I became depressed. I felt inadequate and ashamed. For the first time in my life, I thought seriously about suicide."

Since Will's political career was no longer a refuge from his inadequacy, he thought about returning to his sexual pursuits to get some relief. "I couldn't believe I was considering getting involved in the very behavior that brought me down. I felt like an alcoholic who drinks to drown his sorrows from his drunken behavior the night before."

Will's story is typical of the life of a sexual addict. He struggled with being in therapy and wanted to try to do it by himself. Covert incest victims resist seeking help because they experience it as a sign of weakness. They often offer help, but seldom are able to receive it. The next story illustrates this more fully.

David, Age Forty-One, Minister

David is a charismatic fundamentalist Christian minister who sought professional help as the result of an order from his superiors. He had made a pass at the wife of a church board member and was accused by another member of seeing prostitutes. His superiors were concerned and did not want a public scandal. They gave David a choice of either losing his ministry or seeking help. Reluctantly, he agreed to counseling.

During the weeks David was relieved of his duties, rumors persisted among the congregation. Accusations increased. A number of women approached church board members to tell their stories. All of them said the same thing: David had attempted to kiss them or coax them into having sex when they counseled with him regarding personal problems.

One woman said she had an ongoing affair with David. She tried to break it off many times, but he found ways to coerce her to remain. With all the rumors circulating about David, she was relieved to have a chance to clear her conscience. The financial secretary also came forward to report large amounts of missing funds that he suspected David had used to support his prostitution habit.

Other members of the congregation couldn't believe it. They thought David was God's messenger and could never commit sexual indiscretions. After all, he preached frequently about sexual promiscuity and spearheaded groups that fought against abortion and pornography.

"Sex," David often preached, "is a sacrament between a man and his wife and a sin between everyone else. Unrepentant sinners will surely perish in the fires of hell." In fact, David's most recent sermons were filled with damnation for sexual sinners.

David's family life was also cited as evidence that the accusations were false. His wife and daughters were never allowed to discuss sexual matters or dress in a provocative way. David was always on the alert for his daughters showing signs of interest in boys or doing provocative things, such as wearing earrings or lipstick. He would correct them and, at times, go so far as to accuse them of being "whores." David was making certain his daughters did not grow up to be loose women. Although David's wife went along with him, she, too, took the opportunity to confide to a church member that he was becoming obsessed with sex. He always talked at home about the sins of sex or raged at her with sexually abusive language. Lately he had begun accusing her of having affairs. She confessed she was beginning to feel battered.

Other church members said David was no different from other men and should be forgiven. "After all, God forgives him, so why shouldn't we? Just forget about it."

It isn't that simple. David is a sexual addict and to "just forgive and forget" helps perpetuate the addiction by not holding him accountable for his actions.

In initial therapy sessions, David was guarded and he denied the reports from the church. After a time, however, he began to confide his story.

I began masturbating at the age of seven to calm myself while my parents fought at night. My father was an alcoholic and often abused my mother. After he abused her he had sex with her, sometimes forcefully. I couldn't understand this. I hated my father and vowed never to be like him. In the morning, after my father left for work, I would go into my mother's room and lie with her. I comforted her while she sobbed. She would say how sorry she was I had to hear the argument the night before and ask me to forgive her. Together, we discussed how terrible my father was. I felt powerful when my mother assured me I was her savior and her only support through the rough times with my father.

David's close relationship with his mother continued, and his contempt and disgust for his father grew. David's own secret

life with masturbation also progressed when he discovered his
father's pornography collection.

> *I began mutual fondling with boys and girls in the*
> *neighborhood. By the time I was an adolescent, I was obsessed*
> *with sex. I was also active in the church and often preached*
> *to my father about immoral behavior. Church was a place*
> *my mother and I went together without my father. The*
> *anticipation for me almost felt like an adulterous romantic*
> *rendezvous.*

Just before David was to go away to a Christian bible college
to study to be a minister, he was accused of getting a high-school
classmate pregnant. He denied it, but she insisted. David's parents
met with the girl's parents, who said she was going away to have
an abortion, and David was forbidden to ever see her again.
David's father was enraged, but his mother protected him and
claimed the girl must be lying.

Privately, David knew the girl had told the truth. Both he and
his mother were relieved he would be going off soon to college.
With a deep sense of shame and disgust for himself, he vowed
he would never do that again and began faithfully to "serve the
Lord." He was a model student, and his instructors assured him
the ministry was his calling. For a while, David refrained from
his sexually addictive behaviors with the exception of compulsive
masturbation, which he decided didn't hurt anyone. Before long,
because his masturbation fantasies no longer entertained him,
he smuggled pornography onto campus. The urge to approach

women sexually on campus grew. He worried that if he got into trouble at school, he would ruin his chance for the ministry, so he began seeing prostitutes off campus. "I reasoned this was okay, because they were just whores and didn't interfere with my work at the school," David explained.

By the time he was twenty-one, David was firmly entrenched in a double life. He had two worlds and was convinced that they did not affect one another. When David's two worlds intersected, he panicked and briefly became conscious of his desperate sexual drive. In one of these moments, he decided he needed to marry a good Christian woman to "put this all behind him." By the time he graduated from college he was married. He promised himself and the Lord—again—that his secret sexual life was over. He had a wife, a clean start, and was about to be appointed minister of a new church. David was certain things would be all right now.

Soon, David was back into pornography and shortly thereafter, prostitution. Another promise and set of convictions had been lost to the addiction. When money ran out, he "borrowed" from church funds. Although they had two daughters, his relationship with his wife had eroded. For years, David kept both lives going. He began feeling tempted by the women he counseled. He was appalled and vowed to never act on this temptation. But as with so many promises before, his will was no match for the "sex-at-any-cost" drive of his addiction. Eventually, he made a pass at the wrong woman, a church board-member's wife, who did not hesitate to confront him and make his indiscretion public. David's double life came to a screeching halt.

Although David did not see it at the time, that woman was

a blessing. There comes a time in the life of all sexual addicts when they reach a point of "hitting bottom," that is, coming face-to-face with the unmanageability and pain of the secret double life. It is at that moment that the addict is offered the chance to choose recovery and sanity. The only alternative is to go back into the denial and rationalization of the addiction and once again hit bottom. Because of the characteristic of tolerance, the next bottom will be more painful and unmanageable than the previous one. For some, however, there are no second chances. Sexual addiction can eventually kill.

David's story has all the characteristics of sexual addiction: secrecy, broken promises, denial and rationalization, tolerance and escalation, and violation of significant core values. David's addiction began, as many do, as a way to medicate feelings— the pain, shame, and rage of witnessing his father's abuse of his mother. The covertly incestuous relationship with his mother began a lifelong emotional bind that left no escape except for the illusion of freedom the addiction offered. The contempt and splitting off from his father and the joining sides with his mother began the development of David's capacity to live in two worlds.

One important aspect of David's recovery was to heal the split he had with his parents. This entailed David's searching his feelings to find compassion for his father, as well as finding the anger and hurt caused by his mother. David could more easily forgive his father than be angry at his mother; it was hard to be mad at a woman who took so much abuse. Yet he willingly acknowledged the rage and shame he felt for being his mother's confidant. He also felt tremendous abandonment from always sacrificing his needs to take care of her.

"It was no accident," David later commented, "that I became a minister." It was a role where he perpetuated the abandonment he felt early in his life. The caretaking of others left him feeling empty. The addiction was an attempt to fill up the emptiness. Abandonment is one of the most significant consequences of the covertly incestuous triangle and one of the main forces driving a sexual addiction.

Another important aspect of David's addiction was the deceptive nature of his public life. His preaching against sexual sins and his activity in antiabortion and pornography crusades was no accident since pornography and abortion were significant sources of shame and guilt in the history of David's addiction. Talking a polar-opposite position such as this is a common psychological defense against shame and anxiety. Freud first referred to this type of human defense mechanism as reaction formation.

It is easy to see how this defense contributes to the double life of a sex addict. Another example is the adulterous spouse who always harshly judges and holds in contempt those friends or acquaintances who have affairs. As the shame, guilt, and anxiety of the secret sexual life increases, so does its opposite behavior. The more extreme, rigid, and self-righteous one is about an issue of morality, the more likely it is that one has something to hide.

David and Ed are high-profile individuals who received immediate public attention for scandalous behavior. This is not to suggest all people with high-profile, public positions are sex addicts and covert incest victims, or that there aren't sex addicts and covert incest victims with ordinary jobs and occupations. Certainly there are.

However, it is important to recognize that the helping and public professions (such as doctors, lawyers, therapists, teachers, clergy, and politicians) do draw covert incest victims into their ranks. After all, these individuals grew up honing the skills that easily transfer to occupations in which giving, saving lives and souls, helping, and achieving are highly valued and rewarded.

The next story is about someone who does not hold a public position, but who is equally invested in the image of high achievement seen in the previous two stories.

Ann, Age Thirty-Eight, Corporate Businesswoman

In the business world, Ann was independent, self-assured, and competent. It was rumored that she was soon to be one of the vice presidents of her corporation. She was always careful never to mix business with pleasure; she never dated anyone from work. Ann was viewed by coworkers as a strong woman. Even though they knew of her three marriages, they saw them as a sign of her independence. She was either envied or held in contempt by the women she worked with, while the men either sought her sexually or were intimidated by her. But no one suspected she had a secret life.

Ann entered therapy because her third marriage was failing. Her husband left her because she was having an affair with a business associate from a different city. This was the second affair her husband had discovered in their marriage. He had had enough. Ann had never sought professional help before, but said:

Maybe I have a problem. I can't seem to be satisfied with just one man. I thought by marrying Gary I would never have to be with another man. He seemed perfect for me, and we had great sex. I can't understand why I did what I did. When I met Gary, I knew he was the one for me. The terrible loneliness that plagued me all my life . . . I was sure it would come to an end. Although I liked being with a lot of men, I was sure I'd be faithful to Gary.

As the weeks passed in therapy, Ann's story unfolded. And Ann did have another life. Though she had a clear rule of not dating the men at work, she actively sought out men who were briefly in town on business. She reasoned they had little or no direct impact on her day-to-day work at the office. She described a recent incident when a man from out of town who was doing business with her company approached her and suggested he had heard she "liked a good time." Ann was appalled. She realized even though she had one image at work, she was developing a different reputation elsewhere. She became paranoid and vowed never to see other men who were doing business with the company. "Besides," she confessed, "I'm not giving my marriage with Gary a chance."

Her resolution didn't last long. Ann met a man she couldn't resist. She reasoned it was safe, because he had done business only once with the company and would not again. Ann also claimed this was different. "He was somebody I really liked. It was more than just an affair. We really experienced intimacy together.

I began to feel torn as to whether I should divorce Gary and be with him."

After a while, Ann became careless. She permitted this man to call more frequently than she felt was safe. Gary soon caught on and left her. Ann felt ambivalent again. "Maybe I really want Gary now. I don't know what to think," she conceded.

Although she was independent at work, her history revealed her dependency on men. Her three husbands, she claimed, said her dependency was like that of a little girl. She hated to be apart from them and became extremely jealous when they wanted to be separate from her. Other times, she accused them of having affairs. She demanded constant attention and love.

Embarrassed, Ann confessed:

I wanted them to love me like my daddy loved me. None of them did. I feel like that's why I've been so disappointed in my marriages. And that's the reason I have affairs. If they had loved me more, I wouldn't have had to see other men. But I always felt disappointed, so I sought other relationships to fill up the emptiness.

As a child Ann had been "Daddy's little girl," and she still was. She adored and admired her daddy and was adored and admired by him in return. Their relationship was special. Ann admitted she couldn't seem to love anyone like she loved her daddy. She was the oldest of four girls who grew up in a family torn by alcoholism and drug addiction. Her mother was an alcoholic and addicted to prescription drugs.

My mother was a Valium junkie who always seemed depressed and was overly dependent on me and my daddy. I had to take care of her and my sisters. I hated my mother. At other times, I felt sorry for her, but not as sorry as I felt for my daddy. I knew he could never depend on her, so I always took special care of him. I filled in for my mother.

I remember he took me on his business trips out of town. He was a chief executive for a big corporation and needed to go on business trips regularly. I stayed in the same hotel room with him and even slept in the same bed at times. But nothing ever happened. He never touched me except maybe to hold me sometimes. I got to go to some of his business meetings with him. I felt so special. I felt he loved me more than my mother. If it weren't for my daddy, I never would have had any love.

This went on until I was an adolescent, and then it stopped abruptly. I felt so abandoned and lonely. I thought my daddy didn't love me anymore. I tried so hard to please him after that; I made sure I got good grades and always dressed up real nice for him when he went on his business trips. But I never got to go again. At the same time, my mother got worse, and our family became more distant. I felt so alone and frightened. I started having boyfriends and being sexual with them by the time I was thirteen. That seemed to be my escape from the loneliness.

Ann began a desperate search to fill the vacuum created by the seduction and abandonment by her father, as well as the neglect from her mother. Here is where Ann's double life and the split in her personality (between being overly independent and dependent) had its beginning. She tried desperately to please and recapture the attention of her father. High achievement in school and dressing like a good little girl didn't work. Her feeling of abandonment grew, and her desperation to find that special love to fill the emptiness escalated. Ann's secret romantic and sexual search began its painful course at the age of thirteen. Even then, she had little control over the direction of her desperation. Any opportunity for innocence during her growing womanhood was robbed from her by the seductive, covertly incestuous relationship with her father. The only attention she ever felt from him was seductive in nature; thus, she acted out overtly what was transmitted covertly at an earlier age.

Ann's story has themes similar to those previously discussed. For example, the nature of her secret life closely resembled the seductive relationship she experienced with her father. Ann became a corporate executive herself, engaging in affairs with men from out of town doing business with her company. The most seductive aspect of the covert incest with her father occurred when he took her out of town on business with him. This is more than coincidence. Again, it is the psyche's way of healing—re-creating similar circumstances in adulthood in an effort to correct the experience and to get the needs met that were unmet in childhood. However, without conscious awareness of the abuse, patterns repeat and repeat.

The pattern that developed in Ann's situation was one of sexual addiction, or more accurately, sex and love addiction. As mentioned previously, this difference is sometimes a matter of semantics. In Ann's case it warrants clarifying.

One way to distinguish between sex addiction and love addiction is to observe that the use of sex by sex addicts is a method to get high or alter mood. The sexual act is a fix for the sex addict, just as taking a drug is for the drug addict. In contrast, someone addicted to love is compelled to pursue intrigue and intensity in the search for love. Being sexual may or may not be part of that pattern. Although there is certainly mood alteration in love addiction, the motivation behind this type of sexual pursuit is to attain love rather than to get high. As already noted, both love and sex addiction can occur in the same person.

Certainly this was the case with Ann. At times, she seemed indiscriminate in her sexual pursuit. At other times, it became her gateway to intimacy. Additionally, her extreme emotional dependency in her marriages and in her romantic illusions reflected her love addiction. Her romantic illusions have their roots in the seductive relationship with her father. Ann was always on the lookout for someone to "love her like her daddy did." She searched for the perfect partner to fill the extreme neediness and emptiness of the lonely little girl inside of her. Ann consequently remained ambivalent regarding intimacy and commitment.

Ann's ambivalence is most apparent in her indecision about whether she should stay in her marriage or in her affair. She believed she was creating intimacy in her affair, which added to her confusion. Although there probably was some degree of intimacy in the affair, it evolved within an illegitimate context, shrouded with secrecy and shame. This added to the bind of ambivalence for Ann. When relationships have their roots in deceit, secrecy, and shame, addicts remain ambivalent and in conflict with themselves. Such relationships have little possibility for healthy growth due to the chronic ambivalence and shame inherent in their secret beginnings.

It is not uncommon to see people leave marriages or relationships for affairs, only to find themselves faced with similar circumstances in the new situation. Only the names and faces are different. In the recovery process from sexual addiction, it is important for the addict to have honest and legitimate beginnings in new relationships. If an addict has to leave a relationship, it is crucial that he become certain that it is the relationship he must separate from rather than his own inner conflict. Otherwise regret, shame, and confusion prevail.

Another aspect that contributes to the ambivalence of commitment is the unresolved grief from previous attachments that is carried into new relationships. This unresolved grief becomes a source of conflict because it inhibits new beginnings, never allowing a legitimate chance for intimacy.

Ann has to resolve her grief and shame before she can be clear about her commitment in her marriage. She will also need to become willing to end her affair, which is bringing her shame due to its illegitimacy. Ambivalence regarding commitment is a common struggle for covert incest victims.

For the covert incest victim, sexual addiction offers the illusion of escape and separation from the seductive parent. Ultimately, the addiction becomes its own trap. The experience of being sexual is one more aspect of their life not in their control. Covert incest victims must first separate emotionally from their parent before sexuality is integrated as a choice rather than a compulsion.

6

༺◦༒

The Struggle to Commit

But illusions are stronger than we might want them to be.

—Henri J. M. Nouwen, *Reaching Out*

A CHILD who has been a parent's surrogate partner suffers a deep emotional wound. The intuitive sense of self that permits the freedom and trust necessary to make constructive choices in relationships is damaged. In its place, an idealistic illusion develops as to what relationships are and what they can provide. Hoping for a perfect partner or relationship often becomes the criteria by which the covert incest victim makes decisions. Covert incest victims long to fill their illusions and have their intimacy needs met. Since perfection is not possible, never feeling satisfied becomes a chronic emotional response in relationships. Consequently, the ability to make a full emotional commitment to a relationship is greatly restricted.

Typically, the intimacy position that the covert incest victim maintains in relationships is one of ambivalence. "Sitting on the fence" or "having one foot in and one foot out of the door, just in case" are common descriptions of this ambivalence. At the core of the ambivalence is wanting desperately to be loved and fearing it at the same time. The mask or outward manifestation of this fear is the search for the perfect partner. Until the core fear is resolved, the attachment to fantasy remains the only means to attempt intimacy. Tasting the sweetness as well as the bitterness of reality is never realized. Relationships become a string of disappointments that never live up to the expectations.

Ambivalence serves as a way to protect. By holding it as a defense, the covert incest victim stays guarded from the threat of being used and trapped again. Fear of being smothered and engulfed is a core part of the ambivalent commitment experienced. The original pain of being exploited by the parent surfaces in relationships with spouses. These feelings are projected onto the partner, and the covert incest survivor pulls back from the commitment. So, as the initial need for further commitment in a relationship grows, the fear of being used again grows as well. Since the boundaries are often blurred between adulthood and the incestuous wounds of childhood, being able to differentiate between one's spouse and the incestuous parent is difficult. Consequently, the feelings of being violated become active. Ambivalence shields the covert incest victim from the threat of further entrapment.

It bears mentioning that the ambivalence serves another purpose. Since the parent demanded devotion and loyalty in the surrogate companionship, the covert incest survivor's primary emotional commitment remains to the parent. Her partner or spouse gets only a part of her as she struggles to juggle the devotion to the parent with the demands of intimacy from a partner. Remaining ambivalent in the commitment allows the covert incest survivor safety from having to break away completely from her parent.

Although the covert incest victim experiences chronic ambivalence in relationships, the beginning of a relationship is often quick and intense. Immediate and total commitment occurs, followed by uncertainty and ambivalence. The tremendous guilt the covert incest victim carries prohibits leaving if the relationship is not working. Instead, she tries to make it right, only to be disillusioned after each attempt. Or if the relationship has potential, the guilt interferes with clearly identifying personal needs and making a legitimate attempt to make the relationship work. Commitment becomes an arena desperately longed for. However, it is an experience that generates fear and confusion.

These hasty and intense commitments are born out of the attachment to fantasy as well as the tremendous neediness experienced by the covert incest victim. Rather than bonding with the person, the bond is to the fantasy that the person represents. Since the fantasy represents the ideal or perfect person, the commitment is immediate. The person may have some of the qualities of a fantasy spouse, but in reality is never seen for who he really is. When the illusions die—as they all do—the commitment struggle surfaces. Now, faced with who the person really is and realizing the vulnerability of committing so quickly, ambivalence sets in.

The other factor that contributes to hasty commitment is the desperate hunger for attachment felt by the covert incest victim. Having been emotionally abandoned in the incestuous relationship, she has a tremendous neediness for love, which consumes her in her search for a spouse. When this neediness is combined with the ongoing illusion or fantasy, the chances of making a relationship choice rooted in reality are minimal. When it becomes clear the relationship will not fill the longed-for intimacy needs, the feeling of abandonment resurfaces. Additionally, the covert incest victim blames herself for the sense of failure and relentlessly searches herself for fault. She hopes if she is scrupulous enough, she will find out what is wrong with her. Then she can change and make the relationship work. Guilt and confusion over her personal needs become pervasive. The pattern experienced with the covertly incestuous parent is repeated.

The guilt and confusion over personal needs leads the covert incest victim to take cues from her spouse to determine the needs in the relationship. Attempting to fill the spouse's needs in hopes of getting one's own needs met becomes a desperate pattern. Resentment, anger, and hopelessness pervade. This pattern has its roots in the covertly incestuous relationship where the sacrifice of personal needs became the means of survival and the hope for love. The identity development of the child—so crucial in developing clear commitments regarding sexuality, needs, values, wants, choices, and feelings—is blocked. The adult capacity for healthy intimacy is lost.

Jim's Struggle with Commitment

Jim's story reflects the ambivalent and painful struggle that covert incest victims have regarding commitment.

> *I was the oldest of five children in my family. My father was an alcoholic and a womanizer. He was seldom at home. When he was, he and my mother fought or were distant with each other. My mother was often depressed and demanding of me. I remember her trying to keep me close whenever she could. I felt guilty and responsible for her. I sort of took over the role of my dad in the house. When I did try to go out with my friends, my mother would often scream at me and hit me. I felt like I always had to take care of her needs.*
>
> *When I became an adolescent, she would comment on my looks or my body. It always felt seductive and icky. Even though I hated it, it also felt good to be so special in my mom's eyes. As I began to date, I found that I was desperate to find a girlfriend so I could get away from my mother, although I felt terrified at the same time.*

Jim felt hurt and abandoned. He was terrified of his mother's rage. Consequently, Jim was set up to be unsuccessful in his relationships with women. A successful relationship would mean leaving his mother behind and potentially igniting her fury.

Despite his fears of his mother's anger, Jim felt desperate for love. He impulsively married Cindy in an attempt to fill the emptiness and to correct and heal this early damage.

I knew after our first date Cindy was the woman I wanted to marry. She seemed stable, clear, loving, and trustworthy. She also had a strong commitment to family life. Cindy was perfect, and I was going to make her my wife, no matter what it took. My life had been a series of disappointing relationships and meaningless sexual encounters. When I met Cindy, I felt ashamed and unlovable. The knowledge that someone like her loved me took away my pain. After all the ups and downs I had in relationships, meeting someone like Cindy was the answer to my prayers.

Cindy's stability was important. I knew she would be consistent with her love no matter what I did. I had never felt loved as a little boy. My mother's love always seemed conditional on what I could provide her. At best, her care of and for me was inconsistent. Cindy was the opposite of my mother. I knew she placed a high premium on love. If I married Cindy, my fear of being abandoned would be over. My dream of a perfect marriage and a woman who would never hurt me would finally be realized.

Though I knew we had some important differences, I fantasized that they wouldn't matter. Loving each other was what was important. In the beginning, I worked hard at pleasing Cindy. I altered my thinking and feeling to some extent so we would have fewer disparities. I was willing to do anything not to lose her love. But soon reality set in. I began to feel resentful. I blamed Cindy, and spewed anger and hate. The very person who was the object of my love became the object of my rage. Our differences became more important and began to matter. Love was not winning out. I felt confused and trapped.

I began to think about finding another woman. But I was married now, and I vowed I would never be unfaithful. I wasn't going to be like my father. But the pull became too strong.

I began a series of emotional affairs that I would take to the edge by almost being sexual. When I realized what I was doing, I would stop, only to start a new emotional affair. Though I resisted actual sexual contact with these women, the energy I spent controlling the urges left me unavailable to my marriage. I became lost in the fantasies about these women and what they could provide that my wife couldn't. Masturbation became my primary sexual expression. Masturbation was the way I made my emotional affairs sexual. My anger toward my wife and the ambivalence about my marriage grew stronger.

Finally, the pain became too great. I wanted to save my marriage and try again to live out my dream with Cindy. I entered therapy. I hoped if I could straighten myself out, I could love and feel loved as I had always wanted. In that period, I got my compulsive sexual behavior and fantasizing under control and started feeling good about myself. But my uncertainty about the marriage grew stronger. Did I want my commitment? Or didn't I? I wasn't sure I wanted to live with her or be without her. I was angry and confused.

Although I had thought Cindy was perfect for me, I struggled to connect emotionally with her. I began to feel the loneliness I had felt as a child. Our differences, which originally didn't seem to matter, were clearly more important than I wanted to admit. My confusion and uncertainty increased.

Jim's anger toward Cindy was about his mother, not Cindy. When the fantasy bond with Cindy collapsed, his anger surfaced. Though he felt Cindy had let him down, it was his mother who had really done the damage. Being with other women was another way he expressed his anger and tried to stay safe. When the boundary between Jim's mother and Cindy became blurred, being with other women provided sanctuary from the potential of feeling abandoned and engulfed again.

Jim's terror had also surfaced. The fact that his sexual expression was primarily through fantasy and masturbation indicated his need to stay in control and remain protected. Though Jim felt he needed to escape, he was careful not to give too much of himself away to these women. Jim's ambivalence reflected the need to not only protect himself from the feelings of the covert incest wound, but also from the reality of the marriage. Jim and Cindy seemed to have important differences that made an emotional connection difficult. Even though he made efforts to love his wife, in choosing someone he was significantly different from, he could remain loyal to his mother by not having a successful marriage. This is an important and frequent dynamic that helps to explain the chronic dissatisfaction that covert incest victims experience in their relationships.

The tremendous guilt and confusion over personal needs that covert incest victims experience prohibited Jim from making a clear choice to stay or to leave the relationship. On one hand, Jim felt guilty when he considered leaving. On the other, he had too much confusion over his intimacy needs to make a legitimate attempt at closeness with Cindy. Jim needed to work at identifying his intimacy needs before he could be clear.

Also, the tremendous emotional dependency on Cindy, left over from Jim's abandonment in childhood, made it difficult for him to make a decision about the relationship. His story reflects the struggle between the needs of the inner child and those of the adult man. Ambivalence escalates when the needs of the inner child become the priority in an adult relationship. Covert incest victims often transfer the leftover needs and issues with their opposite-sex parent to their spouses or significant others. The next section looks more closely at how this phenomenon gives some validity to the notion that we marry our mothers or our fathers.

Who Do We Really Marry?

As we've examined, a covertly incestuous relationship results in many unmet emotional needs for the child. Additionally, unresolved issues regarding guilt, autonomy, and attachment are carried into adulthood. These wounds contribute directly to one's choice in a marriage partner. The notion that we marry our mothers or our fathers is true when you look at marriages of covert incest victims who have not yet healed from their emotional wounds. In an attempt to work out these issues and heal the wounds, they marry people who are emotionally like their opposite-sex parents. The hopes and illusions are so strong that they prohibit the covert incest victim from recognizing that their needs will again go unmet.

Invariably, when covert incest victims are asked if their

spouses are anything like their opposite-sex parents, the response is yes. They list similar qualities that tend to be the very ones these covert incest victims felt injured by with their parents. It is common for them to make comments such as:

- ❏ "My husband is emotionally absent just like my father was. I can't believe it; I thought I married someone different."
- ❏ "She's always making me feel guilty like my mother did. If I want to do something with my friends, I get the third degree. She hates me to have any separate needs from hers."
- ❏ "I feel like I have to take care of him like I did my dad. My husband's just like a little boy, and I'm his mommy. I hate it. I was my dad's parent."
- ❏ "She is always criticizing me like my mother did. I never feel like I'm good enough. I'm always trying to please my wife. It seemed I went right from trying to please my mother to trying to please my wife, who is never satisfied no matter what I do. I can't win!"

When this transfer of needs and issues from the parent-child relationship to the marriage relationship occurs, the capacity for healthy adult intimacy is limited. Sexually and emotionally, these relationships end up feeling like parent-child or brother-sister connections rather than like marriages. These relationships may be passionless or sexually and emotionally volatile. The incestuous bond is created all over again. The separation from the opposite-sex parent never really occurs; instead, the same or similar attachment is transferred to the spouse. Covert incest victims remain little boys or girls in their marriages unless recovery occurs.

Rather than making an adult choice in a marriage, the inner, emotionally wounded child of the covert incest victim does the choosing. It is easy to see how so many unrealistic expectations and illusions are carried into the marriage. The wounded child expects the spouse to be all the parent wasn't, often expecting perfection and unconditional love. However, the spouse is generally more like the parent than not.

Rather than choosing an emotionally mature adult, covert incest victims choose spouses who have been emotionally wounded in childhood. The result is two adults with childlike emotions struggling to be close, instead of two emotionally mature adults striving to be intimate. The quarreling and bickering in these relationships are sometimes like two children; other times, the partners are like parent-child in their interactions. The relationship rarely resembles two adults interacting. Satisfaction is seldom realized. After all, adults create intimacy, children don't.

STILL TRYING TO PLEASE MOM

Dave and Marsha's story highlights the transference of childhood needs and wounds to adult relationships. Initially, Marsha came into therapy to complain about Dave's inability to fill her needs.

He always has his nose in the newspaper or is watching TV. He's so uptight I can't talk to him. I want him to take care of me and love me. But either he can't or won't. He is so insensitive to my needs. He's almost like one of the kids. I feel

*like his parent more than his wife. Our sex life isn't that great,
either. I feel like I'm having sex with my brother. That's weird;
I don't understand it. Sometimes I can't believe I married him.
I wish he were different. I want to feel special and important
to him. But I don't.*

Marsha's complaints were endless. Her extreme focus on
Dave left her little room to look at herself in the relationship. She
was convinced Dave needed to do the changing and growing up.
When I saw them together, their interaction was clearly that of
a parent and a child. Marsha scolded and Dave got defensive or
tried to placate. At those times, Dave was a boy wanting to please
his mommy. When he was able to muster any show of power as a
man, it was done with rage. Then Marsha withdrew and became
silent. In those moments she was a little girl pouting because she
wasn't getting her way. Though Marsha complained of wanting
Dave to be more of a man, she clearly was threatened by it at the
same time.

Dave, on the other hand, seemed stuck in being a little boy.
He described his oldest son as having more power than he did. In
fact, the fighting between Marsha and her oldest son was more
like two spouses than parent and child. Dave and Marsha also
had a daughter who was three years younger than their son. As
they described their relationship with their children, it was clear
that more of the passionate and emotional energy was directed
toward the children rather than toward each other.

For example, it was common for the children to sleep with
their parents, or for Marsha to fall asleep at night in her son's bed

with him, and for Dave to do the same with his daughter. They felt they could receive the comfort and closeness from their children that they struggled to get from each other. Even though some young children may occasionally fall asleep with their parents, it is important that parents consider the age-appropriateness of the child and their own motivations. For example, what is cute and secure at two might be too much at eight. In Dave and Marsha's case, their motivations were self-serving and not necessarily in the best interests of the children. As a result, there were more likely to be problems in the emotional and sexual boundaries with the children, though overt incest was not present. Children are not supposed to be their parents' companions in bed. Sometimes, when boundaries with sleeping arrangements are not appropriate, the overaroused feelings from the covert incest can be acted out as overt incest between siblings.

When Marsha was not in the session, Dave was more open and shared his feelings about the marriage. Even then he was guarded, as if he wanted to protect Marsha and not complain too much.

> *Marsha's got a point. I'm certainly not very open with my feelings. I try to accommodate her and meet her needs. I tell you, if it wasn't for her telling me that I wasn't intimate, I probably would never be able to be close. I really depend on her to guide me in the relationship. But there are times when I get mad at her. Although she may be right, she never lets up. She even criticizes me in front of my friends. And I just sit there and take it. I'm afraid if I get angry, she'll shut down and won't*

talk to me for days. She is so damn controlling. It's like she wants me to be open with my feelings, but on her terms—and that doesn't include being angry with her. I don't think I'll ever please her. Frankly, I'm getting fed up with her complaining.

I have to admit, I feel like a little boy around Marsha. I hate it, but I don't know how else to be. It's almost like being around my mother, always trying to please her and be her helpful little boy. I'm afraid if I start being more of a man around Marsha, we won't have much of a relationship. Sometimes, I just want to put her in her place and tell her to knock off the criticizing and complaining. But I'm afraid I'll lose her love. She's so much like my mother! Whenever I was even a little disobedient, my mother took away her love and approval.

As time went on, Dave talked more about his family. Clearly, he was trapped in a covertly incestuous relationship with his mother. He was the youngest of three boys, and his mother kept Dave at her side all his growing-up years. He was mother's good little boy and helper. As he described his incidents of disobedience as a child, it was apparent they were attempts at autonomy and not behavior reflective of a bad kid. However, his mother opposed any separate behavior and was critical of him as a way to control his separateness. This left Dave feeling guilty about his desire for independence. Dave had been abandoned by an alcoholic father, and he relinquished his attempts at separateness to avoid being abandoned by his mother, too.

Dave was a good kid growing up, never causing any trouble. He did whatever he had to do to please his mother. Instead of going out with his friends after school, he went home and helped clean the house. He hated that, but thought he should do it. Clearly, Dave was controlled by tremendous guilt and a deep sense of shame that left him feeling unworthy of his desire for separateness.

Then Dave met Marsha. Marsha was such a nice girl that his mother approved. Privately, Dave knew marrying Marsha was his only way to get away from his mother, so they married early in the relationship. But Dave never left his mother emotionally. Instead, he essentially married his mother by re-creating the same emotional relationship system with Marsha. There are many parallels between Dave's mother and Marsha, particularly the women's critical attitudes and the way they used Dave to fill their own needs without considering his.

Dave's mother used Dave to fill her need for a husband. Marsha not only wanted Dave for a husband but wanted him to fill the needs not met by her father. Marsha's father was distant, cold, and preoccupied—much as she described Dave. There actually were intimacy problems between Dave and Marsha, but her chronic complaining and never feeling satisfied were more likely about her father.

Dave and Marsha married their parents in each other. They also passed on to their children inappropriate sexual and emotionally passionate energy—energy meant for each other. Since Marsha and Dave were both children emotionally, an intimate adult connection was a struggle. Connecting with their children became a primary means of experiencing intimacy. The children, in turn, learned that boundaries regarding privacy and safety could be crossed. This is an example of how incestuous relationship dynamics are passed on from one generation to the next. Dave and Marsha both needed to separate emotionally from their parents to correct the boundary problem with their children and have a chance at intimacy with each other. The process of separating from parents and getting needs met are discussed in Chapter 7, "Moving Forward."

Does this mean that just because you married someone like one of your parents, you should get divorced? No. But it does mean you have to grow up emotionally to resolve the struggle with commitment and to feel satisfaction in your marriage or relationship. It means both people have to be emotionally mature for intimacy to occur. If only one is, the relationship deepens in its parent-child feeling and becomes further removed from the chance of a gratifying partnership.

Marriage should be a celebration of intimacy, rather than an attempt to fill the illusions of the abandoned inner child. It is important for covert incest victims to stick it out in relationships long enough to make sure they are divorcing the right person. Too often, the covert incest victim jumps from one marriage or relationship to another. This is an effort to separate from the leftover emotional bind with the parent, rather than to clearly decide whether the current relationship is not working.

Who Do We Really Divorce?

Another common relationship pattern for covert incest victims is to leave relationships too early. When things don't work out as expected, or when covert incest victims begin to feel too close, they leave the relationship. They quickly begin to feel dissatisfied due to their illusions about love and romance. They also fear engulfment, and they struggle to sort out how to hold onto their self while in a committed relationship. They don't stick around long enough to work things out and establish a mature relationship. Instead, they divorce one partner and marry the next, expecting things to be different each time. However, changing partners does not change the inner reality of the covert incest victim.

This pattern is the struggle to remain committed. Covert incest victims never stay long enough to move from the attachment to the fantasy (or perfect) person to the reality of the individual. Instead of trying to bridge genuine intimacy, they bolt from the relationship, looking to bond with a new person but the same old illusion. They successfully avoid the feelings of engulfment and smothering they carry from their childhoods, but fail to stay long enough to work through them so they can finally separate emotionally and sexually from the memory of the intrusive parent.

Covert incest victims need to stay long enough in relationships to allow the illusion to die and to permit legitimate intimacy to develop. Until this occurs, chronic unhappiness and discontent remain. Covert incest victims often find themselves wondering if the relationships they abandoned would have worked if they had just "stuck it out." This adds to the ambivalence and makes it more difficult to commit to a new relationship.

The underlying issues of separation and attachment are *never* worked out when a covert incest victim gets divorced and jumps from relationship to relationship. Though poor choice in partners can be the underlying reason for multiple relationships, it can be equally true that the person who leaves is running from an inner struggle, based on the fact that separation from the opposite-sex parent has never occurred. Thus, when she becomes involved with someone, all the pain, fear, and rage meant for her parent resurfaces. Rather than dealing with the feelings, she projects them onto her spouse. Her spouse then becomes the object from which separation must occur. In reality, it is the parent who the covert incest victim is attempting to divorce over and over again, not the spouse.

IS DIVORCE INEVITABLE?

Rachel was in the process of her third divorce. She came into therapy because she was having second thoughts about going through with it.

I don't know if I really should do this or not. After all, this is my third marriage in less than ten years. I feel like I'll divorce Alan and find someone else and divorce him. I'm beginning to think something is wrong with me. I sometimes think if I hadn't had so many unrealistic expectations, my first marriage could have worked. I don't think I really ever got over my relationship with George. In fact, I was still involved with him when I started with my second husband. But I did have some space between my second husband and Alan. If there's some way, I'd like to try to work things out in my current marriage.

I don't want to be divorced again, but I have some real problems with Alan. He's too demanding and seems clingy to me. Lately, when he wants to be close I just shut down. I don't want anything to do with him. At other times, I'm furious with him. He can't do anything right. I want something more out of this marriage and some kind of emotional satisfaction that I'm not getting.

Yet, when we do get close, I'm terrified. I don't want to be smothered like my dad smothered me. It was the same with each husband. I get too afraid to get any closer, but then I complain that we're not close enough. I manage to find a way to attack and blame the relationship. Soon, we're fighting too much, and I'm complaining all the time. Then I can't wait to get out. Divorce always seems to be inevitable. I keep hoping my knight in shining armor out there will rescue me. I thought Alan was my knight, but now I can't wait to get away from him. I can't seem to stay committed and satisfied. I don't know what to think.

When I asked Rachel to say more about what she meant by not wanting to feel smothered like she was with her dad, she told her story.

My father always had me by his side when I was growing up. I was his little sweetie. He and my mother didn't have much of a relationship, so I was the object he adored. When I was younger, I enjoyed all the attention and closeness. But when

I got to adolescence, I couldn't stand it. He never liked any of the men I dated, and he always asked me what seemed like an endless number of questions about what I had done on my dates. Even to this day, he's always prying into my personal life.

He never approved of any of the men I married. It's like he never let me go. I really can't stand it. It feels icky to me, like I can't get away. I feel smothered by him. I just want to scream and run away. It's exactly the same feeling I've had with each husband at some point in the relationship. I start to feel smothered and want to run. And I usually do. I guess that's why I keep getting divorced. Sometimes I think all of my complaining is a way to justify my wanting to run from the relationship.

Rachel's story reflects the commitment struggle that leaves covert incest victims regretting past relationships. The regret generally is that the relationship might have worked out if a longer commitment had been established. As Rachel's story reflects, running from the commitment occurs when a relationship becomes too intimate. At those times, the injury surfaces from the incestuous relationship with the opposite-sex parent and abandonment by the other parent. The pain is so great, and the fear so overwhelming, that running becomes an alternative. Without the framework of understanding, the damage of the incestuous relationship—feeling trapped—is experienced as originating from the spouse. Fear of losing what little autonomy and comfort the incest victim established pushes her out the door. Multiple divorces or relationships are the pattern masking this struggle.

Once the withdrawal from the relationship begins, the covert incest victim uses the old illusion of finding the perfect partner to mask the pain and justify the withdrawal. In Rachel's situation, she was looking for her knight in shining armor. Her desire to divorce Alan could have been the beginning of another confusing, regrettable ending. However, divorce was not the best alternative given Rachel's history. Instead, she decided to stay with the pain and abandonment created by the incestuous relationship with her father so she could separate from him. She also needed to let go of the false illusions and expectations, as well as work through the fear of engulfment. Only then could acceptance and reality become the building blocks needed for intimacy. Letting go of the illusion has a grieving process of its own that adds more pain to the pain of the incestuous injury. This is a difficult, but necessary, period for covert incest victims.

Afterward, Rachel was able to work through her struggle enough to commit to Alan and feel satisfied and comfortable, an experience she had longed for all of her life. As part of her process of recovery, Rachel had to say a clear good-bye to George, her first husband. Essentially, she had started an affair with her second husband and never finished her relationship business with George. The unfinished business added to her confusion and inability to commit to Alan. Being involved in affairs adds another false set of realities and expectations to the struggles the covert incest victim has with commitment and a desire for intimacy.

THE FALSE PROMISE OF THE AFFAIR

Becky was dissatisfied in her marriage for most of its duration. She never knew what was normal in relationships and assumed her dissatisfaction was typical. She and her husband were high-school sweethearts who married right out of high school. He always treated her like a princess and was the sort of guy she always dreamed she should marry. Becky's father always treated her like his princess, so marrying Dan seemed right. During her therapy sessions, Becky acknowledged that marrying Dan was the only way she could get out of the house and away from her father.

Becky loved her father's attention when she was young, but as she grew into adolescence, she began to resent it. In fact, his attention became entrapping. She always felt guilty when she wanted to do things with her friends or when she started liking boys. She always felt as if she had to be at her father's side. Her father frequently made comments that left Becky with more shame and guilt. She recalled that when she met boys, her father often commented, "Nobody's good enough for my princess!" When she met Dan, Becky feared her father would not approve. But he didn't disapprove, so Becky stayed with Dan.

Becky described the marriage.

Throughout our courtship and most of the marriage, Dan treated me like a princess the way my father did. He gave me everything I wanted and things he thought I should want. He was there for me at all times and made few demands. The only demand I sensed was an implicit one: "If I treat you this well, you are mine. I own you." Though he never said this to me,

I always felt the expectation. It was the same expectation I felt with my father. I felt controlled. As time went on, I began to resent my husband's excessive attention to me as I had my father's.

Becky entered recovery for adult children when she sensed she had grown up in a dysfunctional family. She soon realized her dissatisfaction in the marriage was not normal. Becky also began facing the fact that her marriage was dysfunctional in similar ways to her parents' marriage. Becky met Frank at one of the adult child meetings and they soon formed a close friendship. They had long talks over coffee after the meeting and talked to each other over the phone between meetings.

I couldn't believe how I was beginning to feel for Frank. He was everything my husband wasn't. I was able to be myself. Frank never put any pressure on me. I was able to communicate and be intimate in ways I never had before. I fell in love with Frank. I eventually divorced Dan and continued my involvement with Frank. However, as time passed, our once free-flowing and intimate relationship became a battle. Frank stopped being the open and supportive person he had been. He became scared and ambivalent. In response, I became desperate and clingy. We often fought without any sense of resolve. I couldn't understand how something so open and loving could turn out to be such a struggle. I felt trapped again, this time by my own desperation and fear of abandonment.

Having an affair is a way to be relieved of the struggle with commitment felt by covert incest victims. The affair becomes a place where they can be open and intimate in ways they have never been before. It is a means to escape the confusion and pain of the primary relationship without having to bring clear resolution. By moving out of the primary relationship into an affair, the original abandonment and separation issues are not engaged. Since commitment is not part of an affair, one's relationship issues do not surface. That struggle remains in the primary relationship, which is why affairs seem so carefree, open, and intimate.

Since one's family-of-origin issues are not engaged, the affair becomes a relationship for which covert incest victims long. It's free of the burden of resolving the commitment struggle. But as reflected in Becky's story, the struggle with intimacy surfaced in the affair once the commitment in her marriage was severed by divorce. Her desperation for intimacy, as well as the feelings of abandonment that were created in the covertly incestuous relationship with her father, carried over from the marriage to the affair. In a different way, Becky felt she had been trapped again. She had been seduced by the affair into believing there was a possible state of burden-free intimacy with Frank. It falsely promised her that she would not have to deal with the drudgery of relating that she had experienced with her husband.

Does this mean Becky should not have divorced Dan? Not necessarily. Does it mean it would have been in her best interest to resolve her issues with her father and her husband first, before moving on to another relationship? Absolutely. Doing so provides clear resolutions and allows healing from the abandonment, which is necessary to begin and maintain healthy and functional relationships. It frees one from having to deal with the possibility of regret for leaving someone with whom you might have been able to work it out. The fact that Becky found herself in the same bind with Frank as she had been with her husband was a heavy burden to carry. So was constantly second-guessing herself about divorcing Dan. Also, she may find herself repeating the pattern of having an affair as a misguided attempt to resolve her inevitable ambivalence. By not resolving her family-of-origin issues, she prevents herself from moving on in life, and instead adds to the ongoing state of ambivalence that covert incest victims experience with commitment.

These stories have shown how critical it is for covert incest victims to separate from their seductive and entrapping parent in order to be able to fully commit to a romantic partner. Only then do successful and loving relationships become possible.

7

❧

Moving Forward

When you get married, 30 percent of your sexual energy
may still be with your [mother] and you got 40 percent for
the woman you're with . . . she's got about 40 percent with
her father and maybe 20 percent left for you . . . that's not
enough.

—Robert Bly, Power and Purpose in Men Workshop, 1988,
Oakland Community College, Farmington Hills, MI

THE PRIMARY TASK for covert incest survivors is to separate from the opposite-sex parent. This is not an easy step and may take years. The fact that so many covert incest survivors remain inappropriately bonded well into their adulthood suggests a tremendous struggle to let go of the parent. This separation will not be given to them. Real emancipation cannot be given to them: it must be taken. Emotional maturity cannot be realized until the covert incest survivors emancipate themselves. One cannot be an adult man or woman and simultaneously hold onto mommy or daddy. For a marriage or relationship to work, full access to one's emotional and sexual energy is necessary. Even then, it's tough. But, as Robert Bly's quote suggests, a relationship cannot fully be functional when leftover sexual energy is tied to the opposite-sex parent.

In their book *The Good Marriage: How and Why Love Lasts*, Judith Wallerstein and Sandra Blakeslee present their findings from interviewing fifty couples who reported happy marriages over many years. They list nine tasks of a successful marriage; the first task on their list is: *Separate yourselves from your family of origin*. The authors claim that in doing so, one is able to invest fully in her own marriage and redefine the lines of connection with both families. Marriages impacted by unresolved covert incest have little chance of accomplishing this task. Because the lines of connection are dictated by the parent's implicit or explicit demands, the spouse ends up in the role of second fiddle. As a result, all other necessary tasks for a good marriage are negatively prejudiced by the failure to invest fully.

The other integral part of the separation is to heal the relationship with the same-sex parent and allow a connection to develop. In fact, this needs to happen to separate from the other parent. Identification and spending time with the same-sex parent is necessary in order to stand separate from the opposite-sex parent and to feel more powerful as a man or a woman.

However, most covert incest survivors have it confused. They are still trying to feel good about themselves by identifying with the energy of the opposite sex. This cannot work. If a man is going to be able to love a woman fully, he needs first to love himself as a man. This begins with his father's love and continues with the support and nurturance of other men. The reverse pattern is the case with a woman, who must bond with her mother and other females to nurture her identity. However, covert incest survivors stay stuck in trying to please the opposite-sex parent, spouse, or partner as a way to feel like a man or woman. (There are different considerations when, for example, the man is gay and has been his mother's surrogate husband. Those issues are addressed in Chapter 8, "Frequently Asked Questions.")

One of the patterns common to covert incest survivors is the seduction and abandonment of the opposite sex. This pattern leaves in its destructive path broken relationships, confused and hurt partners, and lost chances for love. Generally, this is done unconsciously. It is a way to get back at the seductive parent and gain a sense of separateness, control, and power. However, the attempt to break from the seductive parent by seducing and abandoning members of the opposite sex can't work. The separation must be directly from the parent. Following are some suggestions to help you foster the process of separation from the opposite-sex parent and begin healing with the same-sex parent.

Let go of addictions. Addictions rob you of your sense of power and personal authority. They block you from your feelings and your inner reality, which are crucial to the process of recovery.

Get help for your addictions in a specific twelve-step program. Whether you're addicted to sex, food, alcohol, drugs, or anything else, begin by making a commitment to attend a meeting specifically for your major addiction. You will need as much access to your sense of power as you can get to make the separation.

Let go of your idealized image of the seductive parent. Your parent's excess attention to you was largely for his or her own gratification. Acknowledge that the attention you received was violating and abandoning. You will also need to grieve the loss of this idealized relationship. Expect feelings of sadness. Be prepared to deal with contradictions in your feelings for this parent. He or she may have been your only source of comfort in an otherwise neglectful or abusive family system. However, if you insist on only seeing your incestuous parent as "doing the best he or she could," you miss the opportunity to explore the full range of your authentic feelings. You will likely have both positive and negative feelings. This is okay. Learning to manage contrary feelings is part of the maturing process. It allows the development of specific skills that help you manage the disappointments that occur in all relationships.

Acknowledge your anger toward the seductive parent. Find ways to express your anger that are constructive but allow for some discharge of the pent-up energy. For example, you could write a letter to your parent, telling about your anger and your feelings of violation. It is usually best not to send the letter, since it can be harmful—and this is not the goal of your anger. It is also important for you to write the letter without any sense of restriction. You want to feel free to let out as much anger as possible. Knowing your parent will receive it might inhibit you. Writing a letter is a productive way to deal with your anger if your parent is deceased. Go to the grave site and read it aloud. This can be very healing.

If your seductive parent is alive, begin to set boundaries and separate. This is a crucial step. For example, if your parent continues to tell you about personal problems with the other parent, say you are no longer willing to listen. Be prepared to set these boundaries more than once. Long-term boundary problems require a consistent and clear position on your part. Feeling icky, enraged, or burdened by your seductive parent's request or conversation are feeling-cues that you're being drawn into the incestuous role. Respect those feelings and set boundaries. If you feel guilty, which is likely, remind yourself that it is not your job to be your parent's spouse. It is a violation of your boundaries and even abusive for your parent to expect it to be your job. You may need to have no contact at all with this parent for a while. That's okay. Give yourself permission to do so if that's what you need. (For other helpful ideas, see The Importance of Setting Boundaries and How to Set Boundaries sections later in this chapter.)

Deal with your feelings toward the same-sex parent. Again, writing a letter can help. Deal with your anger of being abandoned by this parent and being left to be the spouse for the other. This situation always invokes a deep sense of anger. It is important to differentiate anger from the hate and contempt you feel. Generally, hate and contempt are the feelings that the opposite-sex parent felt toward the same-sex parent and were inappropriately transferred to you. Those feelings needed to be dealt with directly by your parents between each other. You were caught in the middle and carried feelings that were not yours to begin with. Hate and contempt keep you from feeling an attachment to the same-sex parent. Begin to let go of those feelings by acknowledging they weren't yours in the first place.

Spend some time with the same-sex parent separate from your other parent. If this parent is deceased or too abusive to be with, find someone else who can serve as a surrogate or mentor. Often, a sponsor in one of your twelve-step groups can serve this function. You may also have to deal with contradictory feelings with this parent as well.

Learn to manage guilt feelings. Setting boundaries and dealing with your intrusive parent is likely to stir feelings of guilt and disloyalty. Covert incest survivors carry a tremendous amount of inappropriate feelings of responsibility and loyalty to the incestuous parent. Those feelings were inappropriately transferred to you. It was your parent's job to take care of herself (or himself), not yours. Her loneliness and dissatisfaction with her life and marriage should have been discussed with an adult, not with you. Her need for companionship and comfort from her loneliness needed to be filled by an adult, not by you. When you begin to confront burdens, you will likely feel a strong sense of guilt, find yourself minimizing past violations, and declaring loyalty to your parent. Remind yourself that these feelings were placed on you inappropriately. Challenge them and get support.

Get involved in a support group. Here you can talk about your process of separation and receive support. Belonging to a community of fellow travelers helps reduce guilt and sustains you on your journey to independence. Lessening guilt helps break the bond from the opposite-sex parent and supports you in your growing sense of being a man or woman. Often, when turning to family members for help, your relationships with them may become strained. They may have a need to keep your family system intact. You may not get the encouragement you need. (See appendix for a listing of support groups.)

These suggestions are not linear steps, but they reflect aspects of the process necessary for covert incest survivors. In time, as you work through these feelings and set appropriate boundaries, your feelings of love and compassion for your parent may return. You can begin to see your parents as injured adults—as children who did not get their needs met either and were likely violated as well. Forgiving and letting go, so you can get on with your life and create working relationships, is hopefully where your process will take you. It is important that you not forgive too soon. If you forgive before you work through this process, it isn't forgiveness at all, but denial of the truth.

The Importance of Setting Boundaries

Covert incest survivors have not developed a sense of boundaries with others. Since the intrusive parent inverted the parent-child relationship for his or her own needs, the child learned that others' needs are more important. As a consequence, they have not learned how to set a boundary that establishes a sense of separateness with others. They often feel devoted and loyal to others at a cost to themselves. For example, someone may demand something of you that you are uncomfortable with, but you agree to do it anyway since you struggle to say "no" or "I'd prefer not to." Sometimes, these moments of apparent passivity and dependency have significant consequences, like agreeing to a marriage or a job you don't really want. In adulthood, covert incest survivors struggle with expressing needs, wants, and preferences without feeling guilt.

The most critical boundaries you must set are with the parent with whom you have the surrogate companion relationship. These boundaries should focus on frequency of contact, answering phone calls, texting, topics of conversation, physical touch, and money. Some covert incest survivors struggle not to feel "on call" with their parent and not to answer every call as if it is an emergency. In such cases, I encourage survivors to let voice mail pick up the call and then wait twenty-four hours before answering. You may also need to reconsider your participation in social networking (such as Facebook) where your parent will have "access" to you. This can be very difficult because of the guilt that comes from inappropriate loyalty and devotion.

Another important consideration is to begin setting a boundary of having no discussions with your parent about her dissatisfaction in her marriage, her loneliness, or her need for someone to listen. Since marital strife is the most frequent topic that the intrusive parent has burdened the child with, it must be stopped and redirected. You are not supposed to be your parent's companion or counselor. The boundary should also include no refereeing your parents' marital discord. If they fight in front of you and try to draw you in, say "I'd prefer not to be involved or around when you two are fighting. I'll come by later after you work this out." By saying this, you are making it clear to them, and to yourself, that refereeing is not your responsibility. You may have to set similar boundaries with your siblings, who may also try to draw you into "taking care of things."

How to Set Boundaries

In my book *When He's Married to Mom: How to Help Mother-Enmeshed Men Open Their Hearts to True Love and Commitment*, I suggest you make a list of the most challenging boundary issues you face and practice setting appropriate boundaries so you are ready to use them when the time comes. The following is a summary of the steps needed to set boundaries:

- Recognize there is a problem.
- Define new boundaries—not too rigid, not too loose.
- Practice setting the boundaries before actually setting them. Be willing to tolerate the loss, guilt, fear, and shame that may come up when they are set.
- Plan for support after having an encounter around the boundaries.
- Set the boundaries and hold firm.
- Get the support as planned.

(from *When He's Married to Mom* by Kenneth M. Adams, reprinted by permission of Simon and Schuster)

There are many situations that will require you to set boundaries so you can be clear on who you are and what you need and want, in relationship with others. This is the most important part of your healing process, allowing for the unfolding of your true, authentic self as opposed to playing the role that was defined for you by your parent. This new defined self will be the compass that directs you in moving forward in your life.

Relationships

What's clear by now is that covert incest survivors struggle to have a satisfying, committed love relationship. A core issue contributing to this struggle is the confusion resulting from reacting to your spouse as if he were your parent. Developing an inner boundary allows you to distinguish between these two relationships. This is a necessary step to establish a working relationship for yourself. The separation process just described goes a long way toward that end.

In fact, I recommend that you establish a sense of separateness from your parent before you make any major decisions about your relationship. Your emancipation allows you to be more available to yourself and your relationship. If you're single, you'll be more likely to choose a mate based on adult intimacy needs rather than those of the violated and abandoned inner child. If you're considering divorce or letting go of a relationship, the separation process helps make it clearer that you are leaving the right person. The following are other relationship considerations that covert incest survivors must make:

1. Let go of your fantasies. Remember, the abandoned and hurt little child inside you has likely created a rich fantasy life about love, sex, and romance as a way to cover your pain. If you continue to attempt to create adult relationships out of your fantasies, you will add to your sense of abandonment and your chronic feelings of dissatisfaction. Keep working toward acceptance of the reality of yourself and the reality of your partner. You stand a much better chance at establishing a workable relationship. Allow yourself to grieve the loss of your fantasies and illusions.

2. Learn to identify and manage your projections. Covert incest survivors often project feelings toward their parent onto their partner or spouse. For example, a spouse may innocently want you to check in while on a business trip, and you may react angrily, as if it were your parent making demands. Own your feelings from the past, and be responsible for their expression. Do not put them onto your spouse; they will create distance with her and keep you loyal to your parent. The ultimate declaration of loyalty to your demanding parent is to shield her from your true feelings and never have a successful romantic relationship.

3. Make a full commitment to stay in your relationship if you judge it to be good for you. Separate the insatiable needs of the inner child from the realistic intimacy needs of the adult. Regrettably, all the developmental needs lost to the incestuous relationship will not be met fully in any one partnership. The sooner you accept that, the less likely your victimized inner child will project demands that

are inappropriate to adult relationships. Those demands destroy relationships that might otherwise be good for you.

4. Burn your bridges. One of the patterns that contributes to relationship ambivalence is keeping a couple of relationships going at once, or "keeping the door open" on past relationships—just in case you have to make a run for it. The underlying fear behind fully committing is, "I will be used and betrayed again, as I was with my incestuous parent." At stake is the fear of losing your sense of self in the relationship. Additionally, you avoid deep feelings of pain and anger by keeping yourself in this pattern.

   If you are going to resolve your ambivalence toward commitment, you need to burn your bridges by letting go of relationships that are designed to keep you on the run; that may mean *no contact*. You also need to grieve the loss of those relationships. Remember, you deserve a healthy and intimate love relationship with one person— and you are capable of one. But you have to let go of old, self-destructive behavior patterns before you can be open to intimacy.

5. Set boundaries and make your personal needs a priority in your relationship. The fear of losing yourself in a relationship is usually founded in truth. The incestuous relationship teaches you to sacrifice your needs in adulthood for the love of your partner. Though this is needed at times in all relationships, you may experience a loss of choice and do it chronically, hoping that maybe your needs will finally be met. This doesn't work, and the seeds sown for deep

resentment eventually help erode the relationship.

It's okay to do what's good for you and not be concerned with pleasing your partner all the time. Boundary setting needs to be concrete, even though you fear it will displease your spouse. You must begin to develop a tolerance for allowing your spouse to be angry or displeased with you. If not, you'll stay stuck in the incestuous pattern of trying to please in the hope of getting your needs met. At this juncture, it is no longer your parent betraying you—it is self-betrayal.

You're likely to feel guilty in these attempts. Your guilt is the result of being violated in the incestuous relationship. Allow yourself to be outraged over being burdened with so much guilt. Your sense of outrage helps you set boundaries. Adults who grew up with functional parents who did not use them to gratify their own needs do not feel enormous guilt when the adult child attempts to get their needs met.

6. Say good-bye to your relationship if necessary—even after all this work. Not all relationships work. You may discover at some point that it is not your parent you're attempting to leave or are dissatisfied with, but your spouse. As you come into your own sense of self and gain some perspective, you may realize your relationship is not good for you. Again, your sense of guilt may be tremendous. You may want to hang on so as not to hurt the other and to avoid dealing with feelings of abandonment. If leaving is what you need to do, you are not a bad person.

Your sense of outrage at being in another guilt-ridden

bind may be what you need to have the presence of mind to let go. At the same time, it is important not to act out this outrage against your spouse by blaming or attacking. Don't be a victim by thinking, "This has happened to me again, and it's my spouse's fault." Take responsibility for your choices, feelings, and decisions. If you don't, you will have a larger blind spot when it comes to the intimacy traps in your next relationship.

7. Watch your seductive behavior. Keep your seduction in check. You don't do yourself or anyone else any favors by engaging in behavior that results in hurt, confusion, and emptiness. Remember, your pattern of seduction and abandonment is a way to experience feelings of power and control intended to help you overcome the sense of victimization as a child. But it doesn't work. If your seduction is part of a pattern of sexual addiction, get some help.

Seductive behavior also has the purpose of hurrying relationships along to avoid your underlying fears and fulfill your fantasies. The seduction greatly distorts your sense of reality of the relationship and of the person you are involved with. Once reality comes into focus, you may begin to withdraw because you realize you have gone too fast and have become too vulnerable, or you may realize that this is not somebody with whom you should be vulnerable. By all means, when beginning new relationships, go slow, stay rooted in reality, and allow the relationship to unfold as it should, not as you would attempt to control it.

Dating

If you are not in a relationship and are beginning to date, there are important considerations for you as you begin your journey. Because the parent demanded excessive loyalty and devotion, covert incest survivors often declare loyalty and commitment quickly, even if they do not want to be with the person. They may also get involved or marry someone who re-creates the parent-child bond—a spouse or partner who is demanding, possessive, and never satisfied. They have a hard time sorting out who will be best for them in a dating situation because they often get "involved" rather than date. They create quick and unhealthy dependencies rather than develop successful partnerships.

Dating is meant to be a sorting-out process, a time to slowly get to know someone to see if that is the kind of person or relationship you want to develop. Make a list of characteristics you seek in a mate and use it has a guide. You should also make a list of boundaries—under what circumstances you should be sexual, how many times a week to have contact, how often to phone or text, and so forth. The more you can hold to a set of boundaries that keeps you from quick dependencies, the more likely you are to create a successful partnership when you are ready and to lay a foundation that helps keep the fear of commitment in its place.

Loving Yourself

One of the consequences of being victimized is feeling objectified and used, not loved. As a result, you also relate to yourself and others as objects to be used. You probably struggle to believe you are worthy of being loved. This makes committing to and loving someone else difficult. Learning to value yourself as lovable is an important part in your ability to love someone else.

A committed relationship is about building and nurturing an enduring love between two people. Because you were never nurtured by your parent, you may have difficulty receiving love and nurturance. Or, you may resent giving love and consequently hold back.

Your journey of recovery needs to include learning to develop a tolerance for self-love. You do this by making simple statements of affirmation on a daily basis. For example, "I love myself unconditionally" is a place to start. You might try this while looking into your eyes in the mirror. You can develop any number of statements to affirm your feelings of self-love. You can also increase your tolerance by doing more acts of self-nurturing, such as cooking your favorite meal, going to a favorite restaurant, walking, talking to friends, taking a warm bath, reading a good book, and so on. Do more of whatever makes you feel a greater sense of self-love, provided it doesn't become self-destructive. (For example, eating disorders and sexual addictions begin as ways to nurture but become self-destructive.)

Another core injury is the damage caused by never learning to trust your own intuitive sense. The covertly incestuous relationship never permitted you to know and trust in your feelings because you were so preoccupied with your parent's feelings. The inappropriate dependency inhibited you from taking personal risks crucial in developing trust in your intuition.

As a child, you needed your parent to provide a safe haven

where you would be nurtured when you took personal risks of autonomy. The incestuous relationship prohibited that from occurring. Your parent needed you too much to permit you the freedom to take risks. Being robbed of the freedom of autonomy is what interferes with developing trust in your intuition. Not trusting your instincts is a crucial factor in creating ambivalence about commitments. Ultimately, you need to be able to trust your gut feeling about a relationship to know what is best for you. When you mistrust this, you may overrely on your intellect. This can distort your intuitive sense. The split between the two helps create the agony of ambivalence.

Begin teaching yourself to take risks and to trust your intuitive sense. Begin with small issues and decisions—base them on your gut feelings. Keep practicing and returning to this process. Remember, it is okay to do what is right for you.

Finally, keep nurturing your abandoned inner child. No one else can do it for you. Carry a picture of yourself as a child or hold an image in your mind and look at it daily. Tell your child all the things he needed to hear but didn't. Reassurance. Affirmation. Encouragement. You deserve it!

8

‿∞‿

Frequently Asked Questions

*Be patient toward all that is unresolved in your heart and try
to love the questions themselves . . .*

—Rainer Maria Rilke, *Letters to a Young Poet*

DURING MY LECTURES and therapy sessions, I have
frequently been asked many questions that I would like to
address in this chapter. It is a chance for me to clarify aspects of
covert incest that may not have appeared in the text. I hope that
this added discussion furthers your healing journey.

I acknowledge that many of you are looking for answers as you
proceed with certain aspects of recovery. I will attempt to clearly
answer certain questions to provide you direction; however, do

not underestimate the questions themselves. The fact that you are questioning your relationship with your parent means you are bringing about awareness and activating the process of change in yourself. By increasing your awareness, your own intuitive healing journey has begun. Trust in time for answers that are not yet clear, and love the questions themselves.

Q *Isn't it good to be close to your parents while growing up?*

A Yes, absolutely it is. When the relationship is primarily based on the needs of the child, children are free of the burden of inappropriate guilt and obligation to the parents. This early attachment becomes the gateway to successful adult relationships. Children are able to trust their own instincts and know their needs, which enable more healthy choices in friends and romance. But in a covert incest relationship with a parent, being close means feeling excessive responsibility toward the parent. Children lack the freedom needed to know their own needs and desires. The parent's needs become incorporated as their own. Constantly torn between demands from the parent and their own wishes, children learn to sacrifice themselves to satisfy the parent and temporarily escape the burden of excessive guilt and anxiety. This becomes a path to frustration and disappointment in adult relationships, particularly in romance. In the case of covert incest, being close with your parent is not in your best interest.

Q *How can a relationship with a parent be considered incestuous without actual sexual contact?*

A This is an important question. Many people are confused by the concept that a parent who uses a child as a surrogate partner, even without sexual touch, still crosses incestuous lines. When we think of incest, most people think of being sexually intruded on and violated, which results in having sexual (and other) problems in adulthood. In a covert incest relationship with a parent, the child becomes the companion and trusted "lover." Children feel icky, too close, and enmeshed in the adult world of the marital and sexual frustrations of the parent. In adulthood, they do not feel free to sexually pursue the "love of their life"; they must declare loyalty to the parent. Their own sexuality is encased in overstimulation, confusion, and feelings of disloyalty. They are more likely to create a sexual fantasy world in which to retreat than to boldly pursue a partner of their own choosing. They become their parent's emotional or psychological lover and companion. Here, no physical touch was necessary for sexuality to be intruded on and violated. They are victims of covert incest.

Q *Can someone experience both covert and overt incest with the same parent?*

A Yes, someone can play the role of a surrogate companion and also be sexually violated by the same parent. There are some different results for the victim between the two roles. Overt incest victims often report intrusive smells, touch, and other sensory recollections (described as flashbacks) that intrude on daily functioning. Overt victims tend to feel more lost, having had to create compartments or different aspects of themselves in order to survive the overt incest. On the other hand, covert victims tend not to report the same level of compartmentalization or intrusive recollections. They will report being stuck playing a role in life, struggling with expressing their true selves. They mistake their roles for their identities. In this sense, the role has become a compartment used to survive. Both overt and covert survivors will report feeling engulfed and smothered by the parent. Recovery requires attention to both issues if they have occurred to the same person.

In some instances, a mistake that incest survivors and professional therapists make is to treat the surrogate partnership role as a minor issue compared to the overt incest. They may also assume the presenting problems are only a function of the sexual touch and subsequent violation. Some survivors will report the direct sexual touch as only a brief part of the ongoing overt-covert relationship. The covert incest aspect, and its damaging effects, may continue for years after the overt touch as stopped. Throughout the therapy and healing process, it is critical that both be thoroughly explored for recovery to have its most useful impact.

Q *My mother was the only parent there for me. I feel so guilty thinking of having my own life. How can I abandon her?*

A The goal of recovery from covert incest is not to abandon your parent. The purpose is to reestablish relationship boundaries, define your level of participation, and identify your needs. Feeling guilty about leaving your parent behind as you live your own life is common.

Let's clarify some of the issues here. First, one of the duties of parenting is to have children who eventually leave and lead their own lives. A parent who entrapped you in the role of a surrogate husband or wife has burdened you with excessive feelings of responsibility and guilt about their marriage or their life; those are not your responsibility. Those problems are not your fault and not something for you to solve. Second, you are not abandoning them. Adults are responsible for themselves. Certainly, elderly parents need assistance from loved ones, but the covert incest burden is different. Covert incest is designed to prevent you from leaving. It is critical that you begin to see the trap you are in and challenge the guilt you carry. Your ability to have an independent life and a successful romantic, sexual relationship depends on it.

Q *How do I set boundaries with others without them feeling hurt or being angry with me?*

A Reestablishing how much and the way you participate with your parent, siblings, friends, and spouse or partner will be necessary. Setting boundaries around topics of conversation and time spent together are common places to start. You will need to tell your parent that you are no longer available to them on an "on call" basis, and that your priority is your spouse. You may also need to tell your siblings that you don't want them being the messenger for your parent who is not happy that you are setting new boundaries. Your role as caretaker with friends, and even your spouse, will likely need to change. You will want to assert preferences and opinions that begin to reveal more of your true self. Yes, your friends and family may not understand and may even feel hurt or angry that you are changing the relationship.

This will be particularly true for your parent, with whom boundary setting is critical to your ability to have your own life. Setting boundaries with others does not require their consent and understanding. Don't leave it to others to grant you freedom to state your needs!

Q *I can't seem to make a decision for myself or state opinions. Is that common with covert incest survivors?*

A Yes, it is. In healthy family systems, we develop a sense of our needs, wants, and preferences by being validated and seen for who we are. We carry into adulthood a feeling that we have value that allows us to stand up for ourselves, state opinions, and make decisions that are in our interest without feeling unnecessary guilt. In the covert incest relationship, your identity was dependent on organizing around your parent's needs and validating her. Little validation was available to you unless it served the needs of your parent. You would have learned early on to experience others' needs as yours, leaving it difficult and confusing when needing to sort out decisions for yourself.

Q *Why is it so hard for me to commit to a romantic partner?*

A In covert incest, your parent treated you like her companion and needed your devotion and loyalty in order to avoid her own emptiness and loneliness. You became the preferred partner over your other parent. This special and privileged position likely felt empowering, but at a terrible cost. When it came time to seek out your own lover, you likely became aware of the conflict about feeling free to do so. Torn between your natural desire to find love and your parent's need to keep you close, commitment to a lover of your choice became a struggle. You likely sought out a compromise, giving some, but not all, of yourself to a lover. This arrangement usually results in loss and disappointment. You keep your parent, but lose your lover. You must confront in yourself the bind you experience and come to terms with whose life you plan to live out—yours or your parent's.

Q *I can't stop my womanizing. Is it related to my covert incest with my mother?*

A There is more than one dynamic behind why men womanize. In the case of covert incest, it is a causative factor. A critical dynamic is your need to constantly re-create the covertly incestuous feeling that you are the special one by repeatedly gaining women's attention. This feeling is quickly satiated with womanizers, and they must move on to the next conquest. Also, if you have been your mother's companion, you probably carry a great deal of anger along with a desire to push away and reject your mother. Unable to do so with mom, you do it with successive lovers. You most likely take the solicitous and attentive behavior you learned with your mother and treat each new woman like she is "the one." The women feel adored and charmed by your attentive behavior, but then confused and at fault when the relationship ends for no apparent reason. When you encounter your own buried conflict around loyalty to mom and your fear of being trapped and engulfed, you abandon the lover to find a new one. This pattern gives you an illusion of freedom that you cannot have with your mother—the ability to reject and declare disloyalty. These patterns can often be addictive. One's efforts during recovery from sexual addiction become a critical part of the healing process.

Q *Are there different issues for a gay man who has had a covert incest relationship with his mother?*

A There are many similarities for gay and straight men who have experienced covert incest, such as feeling excessive guilt, struggling with clarifying needs, feeling overly responsible for others' problems, fearing engulfment, avoiding commitments, and sexual problems and compulsions. One difference lies in the fact that a gay man may identify with his mother and not feel it as an intrusion to his identity. He might be her "friend" in a very normal sense and not feel as compelled to separate from her as the straight man might. Yet, it is critical that he be emancipated from her and that the relationship is not used to replace his father. He must also look to identify some with his father. This doesn't mean he has to embrace the image of the macho man, but clearly knowing and accepting himself is crucial to fully investing in his life and his romantic relationships. He may be his mother's loving son, but he must become, first and foremost, his own man. A last point of clarification concerns the worry some gay men have that their enmeshed relationship with their mother caused their homosexuality. There is no evidence of this. Many heterosexual men have had the same type of relationship with their mothers and are erotically attracted to women. Similarly, if a heterosexual man struggles with approaching women and being sexual, it is not a sign that he is gay. It is more a function of the emasculating feelings and avoidant behaviors that resulted from the covert incest. In general, there are more similarities than differences between the gay man and the straight man who have both experienced covert incest.

Q *Are there any differences when a daughter is the surrogate companion to her mother?*

A Yes, there are. A woman is more likely to come in for help under the auspices of codependency without identifying the surrogate companionship as a factor in her codependency. In fact, the covert relationship with her mother is where she learned to value someone else's needs and feelings over her own, make someone else's problems hers, and feel of value only when she can "be there" for someone. Also, although there is no overt sexual tension between mother and daughter, she will still have the same issues of being unavailable for a full commitment to a romantic and sexual partner. She will fear engulfment as well. She will most likely take on her mother's anger, mistrust, and contempt for her father and then transfer that to other men. This makes it difficult for her to navigate a love relationship with a man successfully. She finds fault with men and stays loyal to her mother.

Eating disorders are common here, too, especially compulsive overeating. Like sexual addiction, it is a misguided attempt to declare freedom—"You can't trap me! I can eat anything I want!" A daughter who has been her mother's surrogate husband must separate from her. This means declaring freedom by not participating in the role of surrogate husband or companion, reestablishing the boundaries of participation, detaching from feelings and perceptions about her father that belong to her mother, recovering from her compulsive or addictive issues, resolving to make her needs a priority in relationships, and claiming the desire for romantic and erotic love.

Q *I tried avoiding men like my father all my life, but I seemed to have picked another just like him—demanding, jealous, controlling, never satisfied, and always making sexual remarks toward other women. This time I married him. How did that happen?*

A In contrast to covert incest survivors who avoid entering romantic relationships, some survivors feel compelled to commit quickly to romantic or sexual overtures. Even when there are warning signs or troublesome behaviors about the man, a sense of obligatory guilt compels you to try to understand and to "make things work." Unconsciously, you have re-created the relationship with your father by finding a man who is controlling and sexually inappropriate. This choice may be part of a larger pattern of choosing men who offer intrigue and having less interest in men who would be more stable. You may hide your own ambivalent feelings about commitment by choosing a man who has more obvious trouble with loyalty and commitment. Until you are willing to examine the covert incest with your father, you may be compelled to continue this pattern of re-creating the past. Underlying this pattern may be love- or sex-addiction issues that cause you to override warning signs. This also will need examination and require your willingness to give up your addiction for recovery to occur.

Q *I am married to a man who is his mother's surrogate husband. I am always second to her when he sorts out his priorities. How can I get him to see that he is hurting our marriage? How do I decide to stay or go?*

A First, unless he is willing to see that there is a problem in his relationship with his mother and seek help, you will likely always feel second choice. It is his responsibility to stand up for you with his mother, set boundaries, and let her know you are his priority. For example, if she makes negative comments about you, he should intervene. However, unless he sees this as an issue he may blame you for being the problem. If you attempt to request changes, try a clear and gentle approach that appeals to his love for you and the desire you both have to make things work. If this fails to motivate him to make changes or to seek help, you have two choices: either accommodate his inability to fully commit to you, with his mother remaining his primary choice, or consider moving on. It is never easy to leave someone you love, but to be second choice after his mother will result in a lifetime of dissatisfaction. You may ultimately need to be prepared with the bottom line of ending the relationship if he can't or won't change.

Q *Is it possible that I could pass on this covert incest to my own children?*

A Yes, it is possible to pass on covert incest to your children. You learned, through your parent's exploitation of you, that it was normal to comfort yourself by turning to your children instead of your spouse. Given your tangled commitment and loyalty issues, you probably find it easier to relate and be intimate with one of your children than your spouse. You may, for example, find yourself overbonded with your child and driving your spouse out of the marriage. Your spouse likely feels tremendous frustration that she can never compete against both your mother and your daughter. As a parent, it is critical that you do not involve your children in your disputes with your spouse or allow them to provide comfort in place of your spouse. Set boundaries with your child by saying, "You don't have to worry about me—your mother and I will work it out. You just go along and play." Be sure to work on the marriage so she sees that the marital bond is primary. A strong bond between you and your wife will bring reassurance to your child and a sense that she doesn't have to worry. Both partners in the marriage must make an effort to invest fully and keep their strong union as the hub in the wheel of the family. Building a strong marital bond will keep your children from feeling compelled to rescue you, and will keep you from using the children for inappropriate comfort. Seek marriage counseling if problems persist.

Q *What if I am a single parent?*

A Single parent families are not necessarily dysfunctional or ripe for inappropriate boundary crossing. However, single parent families may bring a vulnerability to children who are drawn to play the role of a surrogate husband or wife. The empathic, sensitive child will notice your potential loneliness and naturally want to assist or rescue you. This is a normal feeling of love that children feel. They may feel an extra burden to "watch over" you.

I remember doing a radio show with two single mothers as the hosts. After I discussed the subject of covert incest for a while, one said, "Now I know why my adolescent son told me to hurry and get married. He wanted to feel free to go off to college soon." If you're a single parent, make sure you acknowledge your child's love as a positive trait, but seek your companionship needs with adults and provide your child with the message that you will be fine and not to worry. Provide them healthy adult mentors. For example, if you have a son, it is important that he has an appropriate and safe adult male in his life. This should be his father if possible. If your child is inclined to comfort you in your loneliness, reassure him that it is not his responsibility. Give him the freedom to grow up without feeling burdened with your troubles.

Q *I've identified with many of these characteristics, but can I really be happy and content?*

A I like the thought that happiness is a byproduct of a life lived with meaning and not attainable by pursing it directly. By fully investing in our lives and finding meaning, we can certainly be assured of some happiness. The liability for covert incest survivors is that if you are too invested in your parent's life, you cannot invest in a life of your own filled with contentment and happiness. From this perspective, you can see how critical it is that you separate from your parent and from the impact of covert incest. Being in therapy for a period of time will likely be necessary. Covert incest is an insidious process that will require a trained professional to help you steer through the labyrinth of confusion caused by your parent's need to keep you too close. Be sure your therapist understands covert incest and the necessary elements of recovery. Make sure he or she is familiar with the groups listed in the appendix as well as the books in the bibliography. It is important that the therapist neither pushes you to separate too quickly from your parent nor claims that it is "normal" to be so close. Learning to manage your inappropriate sense of guilt, feelings of overresponsibility, and fears of engulfment will provide you with the freedom you deserve to fully invest in your own life and find the contentment and happiness you desire.

Acknowledgments

I AM GRATEFUL for the support and enthusiasm I received from HCI for this new edition, particularly from Carol Rosenberg and Candace Johnson. Candace's skillful editing has made the book more readable. Many of my colleagues have been supportive and encouraging of this book, including Drs. Patrick Carnes, John Friel, Richard Gartner, and Martha Turner, as well as Judith Matheny, Charlie Risien, Carol Ross, and Doug Sorenson. My friends John Bullard, Alexander Morgan, and Carl Schuman have always supported and encouraged my writing. Finally, my wife Cheryl's editing, assistance, and support has been invaluable. I am grateful to them all.

Appendix

The following is a list of organizations that were mentioned in the text of the book as well as others that may be helpful to the covert incest survivor:

Incest and Other Child Abuse

Adults Molested as Children United (AMACU)
P. O. Box 952
San Jose, CA 95108
408-280-5055
www.loveourchildrenusa.org

Childhelp | National Child Abuse Hotline
15757 N. 78th Street, Suite #B
Scottsdale, AZ 85260
800-4-A-CHILD (800-422-4453)
480-922-8212
www.childhelp.org

Incest Survivors Anonymous
P. O. Box 5613
Long Beach, CA 90805
213-422-1632
www.lafn.org/medical/isa/home.html

Parents Anonymous—National Office
6733 South Sepulveda Boulevard, Suite 270
Los Angeles, CA 90045
800-421-0353
www.parentsanonymous.org

Survivors of Incest Anonymous
World Service Office
P. O. Box 190
Benson, MD 21018-9998
301-282-3400
www.siawso.org

Victims of Incest Can Emerge Survivors
(V.O.I.C.E.S.) in Action
P. O. Box 148309
Chicago, IL 60614
312-327-1500

Sex Addiction and the Family

Kenneth M. Adams, Ph.D.
Contact Dr. Adams at
www.sexualhealth-addiction.com, or
www.drkenadams.com

Post your questions for Dr. Adams to answer. Read other people's questions and Dr. Adams's answers. These sites also feature the latest information on sex addiction, covert incest, parent-child enmeshment, and a calendar of workshops, classes, and lectures.

Sex Addicts Anonymous (SAA)
P. O. Box 70949
Houston, TX 77270
800-477-8191 or 713-869-4902
www.saa-recovery.org
Co-Dependents of Sexual Addicts
(COSA)
P. O. Box 14537
Minneapolis, MN 55414
763-537-6904
www.cosa-recovery.org

Society for the Advancement of
Sexual Health (SASH)
P. O. Box 433
Royston, GA 30662
770-541-9912
www.sash.net

International Central Office
P. O. Box 3565
Brentwood, TN 37024
615-370-6062 or 866-424-8777
www.sa.org

S-Anon
P. O. Box 111242
Nashville, TN 37222-1242
800-210-8141 or 615-833-3152
www.sanon.org

Sex and Love Addicts Anonymous
(SLAA)
Fellowship-Wide Services
1550 NE Loop 410, Suite 118
San Antonio, TX 78209
210-828-7900
www.slaafws.org

Codependents Anonymous (CODA)
Fellowship Services Office
P. O. Box 33577
Phoenix, AZ 85067-3577
602-277-7991
www.coda.org

National Organization Against
Male Sexual Victimization
Male Survivor
PMB 103
5505 Connecticut Avenue, NW
Washington, DC 20015-2601
800-738-4181
www.malesurvivor.org

Recovering Couples Anonymous (RCA)
P. O. Box 11029
Oakland, CA 94611
781-794-1456 or 877-663-2317
www.recovering-couples.org

Alcoholism and the Family

Alcoholics Anonymous (AA)
AA World Services, Inc.
P. O. Box 459
New York, NY 10163
212-870-3400
www.aa.org

Alcoholics Anonymous (AA)
General Services Office
468 Park Avenue South
New York, NY 10016
212-686-1100

Al-Anon/Alateen
Al-Anon Family Group Headquarters, Inc.
1600 Corporate Landing Parkway
Virginia Beach, VA 23454-5617
757-563-1600
www.al-anon.org

National Association for Children
of Alcoholics (NACOA)
10920 Connecticut Avenue, Suite 100
Kensington, MD 20895
888-55-4COAS or 301-468-0985
www.nacoa.org

Children of Alcoholics Foundation
200 Park Avenue, 31st Floor
New York, NY 10166
212-949-1404
www.coaf.org

Drug Addiction

Cocaine Anonymous
National Office
P. O. Box 1367
Culver City, CA 90232
213-559-5833
www.ca.org

Narcotics Anonymous (NA)
World Services Office
P. O. Box 9999
Van Nuys, CA 91409
818-780-3951
www.na.org

National Cocaine Abuse Hotline
800-COCAINE (800-262-2463)

Eating Disorders

Overeaters Anonymous
World Service Office
P. O. Box 44020
Rio Rancho, NM 87174-4020
505-891-2664
www.oa.org

For Additional Support Groups

National Center for the
Victims of Crime
2000 M Street NW, Suite 480
Washington, DC 20036
202-467-8700
202-467-8701
www.ncvc.org

National Self-Help Clearinghouse
33 West 42nd Street
New York, NY 10036
212-840-1259
www.mhselfhelp.org

Obsessive-Compulsive Anonymous
P. O. Box 215
New Hyde Park, NY 11040
516-741-4901
www.obsessivecompulsive
anonymous.org

Phobics Anonymous
P. O. Box 1180
Palm Springs, CA 92263

Bibliography

❦

Adams, Kenneth M. "Sexual Addiction and Covert Incest: Connecting the Family Roots of Alcoholism, Neglect and Abuse." *Focus on Chemically Dependent Families.* Pompano Beach, FL: Health Communications, May/June 1987.
———. "Sex Addiction Recovery and Intimacy: The Power of Romantic Delusions." *Focus on Chemically Dependent Families.* Deerfield Beach, FL: Health Communications, June/July 1988.
Adams, Kenneth M., with Alexander P. Morgan. *When He's Married to Mom—How to Help Mother-Enmeshed Men Open Their Hearts to True Love and Commitment.* New York, NY: Simon and Schuster, 2007.
Bass, E., and L. Davis. *The Courage to Heal: A Guide for Women Survivors of Child Sexual Abuse.* New York, NY: Harper & Row, 1988.
Beattie, Melody. *Codependent No More: How to Stop Controlling Others and Start Caring for Yourself.* New York, NY: Harper & Row, 1987.
Bercaw, Bill and Ginger. *The Couple's Guide to Intimacy: How Sexual Reintegration Therapy Can Help Your Relationship Heal.* Pasadena, CA: California Center for Healing, 2010.
Biddulph, Steve. *Raising Boys: Why Boys Are Different—and How to Help Them Become Happy and Well-Balanced Men.* Berkley, CA: Celestial Arts, 1998.
Black, Claudia. *It Will Never Happen to Me!* Denver, CO: M.A.C. Printing and Publications Division, 1981.
Bly, Robert. *Iron John: A Book About Men.* New York, NY: Addison-Wesley, 1990.
Bradshaw, John. *Bradshaw On: The Family.* Deerfield Beach, FL: Health Communications, 1988.
———. *Healing The Shame That Binds You.* Deerfield Beach, FL: Health Communications, 1988.
Brown, Nina W. *Children of the Self-Absorbed: A Grownup's Guide to Getting Over Narcissistic Parents.* Oakland, CA: Harbinger, 2001.
Canning, Maureen. *Lust, Anger, Love: Understanding Sexual Addiction and the Road to Healthy Intimacy.* Naperville, IL: Sourcebooks, Inc., 2008.
Carnes, Patrick. *The Betrayal Bond: Breaking Free of Exploitive Relationships.* Deerfield Beach, FL: Health Communications, 1997.
———. *Out of the Shadows: Understanding Sexual Addiction.* Minneapolis, MN: CompCare Publications, 1983.
———. *Contrary to Love: Helping the Sexual Addict.* Minneapolis, MN: CompCare Publications, 1989.
Carnes, Patrick, with Joseph M. Moriarity. *Sexual Anorexia: Overcoming Sexual Self-Hatred.* Center City, MN: Hazelden, 1997.

Carnes, P. J., and K. M. Adams, Eds. *The Clinical Management of Sex Addiction.* New York, NY: Brunner-Routledge, 2002.

Carnes, Patrick, David L. Delmonico, and Elizabeth Griffin, with Joseph M. Moriarity. *In the Shadows of the Net: Breaking Free of Compulsive Online Sexual Behavior.* Center City, MN: Hazelden, 2001.

Carnes, Stefanie, Ed. *Mending a Shattered Heart: A Guide for Partners of Sex Addicts.* Carefree, AZ: Gentle Path Press, 2008.

Corley, M. Deborah, and Jennifer P. Schneider. *Disclosing Secrets: What, to Whom and How Much to Reveal.* Carefree, AZ: Gentle Path Press, 2002.

Dayton, Tian. *Trauma and Addiction: Ending the Cycle of Pain through Emotional Literacy.* Deerfield Beach, FL: Health Communications, 2000.

Diamond, J. *Looking for Love in All the Wrong Places.* New York, NY: G. P. Putnam, 1988.

Earle, R., and G. Crow. *Lonely All the Time: Recognizing, Understanding and Overcoming Sex Addiction, for Addicts and Co-Dependents.* New York, NY: Simon & Schuster, 1989.

Forward, Susan. *Toxic Parents.* New York, NY: Bantam Books, 2002.

Friel, John and Linda. *Adult Children: The Secrets of Dysfunctional Families.* Pompano Beach, FL: Health Communications, 1988.

———. *The 7 Best Things Happy Couples Do.* Deerfield Beach, FL: Health Communications, 2002.

Gartner, Richard B. *Betrayed as Boys: Psychodynamic Treatment of Sexually Abused Men.* New York, NY: Guilford Press, 1999.

———. *Beyond Betrayal: Taking Charge of Your Life After Boyhood Sexual Abuse.* Hoboken, NJ: John Wiley & Sons, 2005.

Gorodensky, Arlene. *Mum's the Word: The Mamma's Boy Syndrome Revealed.* London, England: Cassell, 1997.

Gottman, John M., and Nan Silver. *The Seven Principles for Making Marriage Work.* New York, NY: Three Rivers Press, 1999.

Grizzle, Anne F., and William Proctor. *Mothers Who Love Too Much: Breaking Dependent Love Patterns in Family Relationships.* New York, NY: Ivy Books, 1998.

Haffner, Debra W. *From Diapers to Dating: A Parent's Guide to Raising Sexually Healthy Children.* New York, NY: Newmarket Press, 2000.

Hendrix, Harville. *Getting the Love You Want: A Guide for Couples.* New York, NY: Owl Books, 2001 (reprint).

Kindlon, Dan, and Michael Thompson. *Raising Cain: Protecting the Emotional Life of Boys.* New York, NY: Ballantine, 2000.

Kasl, C. D. *Women, Sex and Addiction: A Search for Love and Power.* New York, NY: Ticknor & Fields, 1989.

Katehakis, Alexandra. *Erotic Intelligence: Igniting Hot, Healthy Sex While in Recovery from Sex Addiction.* Deerfield Beach, FL: Health Communications, 2010.

Lew, M. *Victims No Longer: Men Recovering from Incest and Other Sexual Child Abuse.* New York, NY: Nevraumont, 1988.

Love, Patricia, and Jo Robinson. *The Emotional Incest Syndrome: What to Do When a Parent's Love Rules Your Life.* New York, NY: Bantam Books, 1991.

Maltz, Wendy. *The Sexual Healing Journey: A Guide for Survivors of Sexual Abuse.* New York, NY: HarperCollins, 2001 (revised).

Mellody, Pia, with Andrea Wells Miller and J. Keith Miller. *Facing Codependence—What It Is, Where It Comes From, How It Sabotages Our Lives.* New York, NY: HarperCollins, 2003 (reprint).

———. *Facing Love Addiction: Giving Yourself the Power to Change the Way You Love.* New York, NY: HarperCollins, 1992.

Miller, A. *The Drama of the Gifted Child: The Search for the True Self.* New York, NY: Basic Books, 1987.

———. *For Your Own Good: Hidden Cruelty in Child-Rearing and the Roots of Violence.* New York, NY: Farrar Strauss Giroux, 1983.

———. *Thou Shalt Not Be Aware: Society's Betrayal of the Child.* New York, NY: Farrar Strauss Giroux, 1984.

Minuchin, Salvador. *Families and Family Therapy.* Cambridge, MA: Harvard University Press, 1974.

Norwood, R. *Women Who Love Too Much: When You Keep Wishing and Hoping He'll Change.* New York, NY: Simon & Schuster, 1985.

Nouwen, Henry J. M. *Intimacy.* San Francisco, CA: Harper, 1981.

———. *Reaching Out: The Three Movements of the Spiritual Life.* New York, NY: Doubleday, 1975.

Osherson, S. *Finding Our Fathers: How a Man's Life Is Shaped by His Relationship with His Father.* New York, NY: Ballantine Books, 1986.

Payson, Eleanor D. *The Wizard of Oz and Other Narcissists: Coping with One-Way Relationships in Work, Love and Family.* Royal Oak, MI: Julian Day Publications, 2002.

Peck, M. S. *The Road Less Traveled: A New Psychology of Love, Traditional Values and Spiritual Growth.* New York, NY: Simon & Schuster, 1978.

Schaeffer, Brenda. *Is It Love or Is It Addiction?* Center City, MN: Hazelden, 1997.

Subby, Robert, and John Friel. *Co-Dependency and Family Rules: A Paradoxical Dependency.* Pompano Beach, FL: Health Communications, 1984.

Trachtenburg, P. *The Casanova Complex: Compulsive Lovers & Their Women.* New York, NY: Simon & Schuster, 1988.

Wallerstein, Judith S., and Sandra Blakeslee. *The Good Marriage: How and Why Love Lasts.* New York, NY: Warner Books, 1996.

Weiss, Robert, and Jennifer Schneider. *Untangling the Web: Sex, Porn, and Fantasy Obsession in the Internet Age.* New York, NY: Alyson Books, 2006.

Wegscheider, S. *Another Chance: Hope and Health for the Alcoholic Family.* Palo Alto, CA: Science and Behavior Books, 1981.

Whitfield, Charles L. *Boundaries and Relationships: Knowing, Protecting and Enjoying the Self.* Deerfield Beach, FL: Health Communications, 1993.

Woititz, J. G. *Struggle for Intimacy.* Pompano Beach, FL: Health Communications, 1985.

Index

❦

About the Author

∽◦∾

KENNETH M. ADAMS, Ph.D., is a licensed psychologist and the clinical director of Kenneth M. Adams and Associates in suburban Detroit, Michigan. In addition to maintaining an active clinical practice, Dr. Adams is a national lecturer, workshop leader, and consultant in the areas of childhood abuse, dysfunctional family systems,, and sex addiction. He is a Certified Sex Addiction Therapist (CSAT), a CSAT supervisor, and a CSAT training facilitator as well as an Eye Movement Desensitization and Reprocessing (EMDR) practitioner. A member of the American Psychological Association, Michigan Psychological Association, Society for the Advancement of Sexual Health (SASH), and International Institute for Trauma and Addiction Professionals (IITAP), Dr. Adams is also an advisory board member to SASH and IITAP, and an editorial board member of *Sexual Addiction & Compulsivity: The Journal of Treatment and Prevention.*

Dr. Adams, along with coauthor Don Robinson, received the 2001 Reader's Choice Award for "Shame Reduction, Affect Regulation and Sexual Boundary Development: Essential Building Blocks in Sex Addiction Treatment," the article voted by subscribers of *Sexual Addiction and Compulsivity: The Journal of Treatment and Prevention* as the Article of the Year. He also received the 2011 Carnes Award for outstanding work and research in the field of sex addiction.

In 2010, Dr. Adams was part of a focus group set up to advise the Office of the Director of National Intelligence on developing criteria for security clearances for federal employees. He specifically advised on matters related to sex addiction and personality disorders. Dr. Adams is the coeditor, with Dr. Patrick Carnes, of *Clinical Management of Sex Addiction* and is the author of *When He's Married to Mom*. He does regular speaking engagements and media appearances, including national and local television and radio. For more on Dr. Adams visit www. drkenadams.com.